THE LIFE OF KING GEORGE THE FIFTH

KING GEORGE V. *Born June 3, 1865. Died January 20, 1936.*

𝕹𝖊𝖜𝖘 ✠ 𝕮𝖍𝖗𝖔𝖓𝖎𝖈𝖑𝖊

THE LIFE OF KING GEORGE THE FIFTH

Compiled by

W. J. MAKIN

*Being a Complete Record
of the late King's life
of Seventy Eventful
Years*

With nearly 250 half-tone Illustrations

London
GEORGE NEWNES LIMITED
Southampton Street, Strand, W.C.2

Made and Printed in Great Britain by
Hazell, Watson & Viney Ltd., London and Aylesbury

CONTENTS

CONTENTS

LIST OF ILLUSTRATIONS

CHAPTER I

DRAMA AT SANDRINGHAM

Illness of George V—Heart Specialists called in—Oxygen brought from London—A Council of State is created—Prince of Wales Motors to London—The Death of the King—Tribute by the Prime Minister.

I

DEATH, when it enters upon the royal scene, does so with the world's limelight upon its fantastic figure. The death of King George V at Sandringham on January 20, 1936, was more dramatic in its effect upon world affairs and the British Empire in particular than any other event since the outbreak of war in 1914.

On Christmas Day, 1935, millions all over the Empire had heard the voice of the King broadcasting his Christmas message to " my dear people." True, there was a real quaver in the voice, a suspicion of tiredness, that many people put down to the deep feeling which the King brought to this Christmas broadcast each year.

Only those who had come into touch with King George during those bleak months of one of the worst winters known to this generation were concerned at the quavering note in the voice. For a few days there had spread a rumour that the King was seriously ill. The rumour was promptly denied. The King himself was seen to walk to church at Sandringham that Christmas. Only the Queen, the Royal Family, and the observant doctor who had recently examined the King, knew that there was some truth in the rumour.

The King's heart, which had struggled so bravely through the long months of his previous serious illness, was at last failing the man who had never spared himself in his duties to the country and the Empire. The death of his sister, Princess Victoria, had come as a shattering blow to a man who had already seen the friends of his youth, intimates of the war years, and men upon whose counsel he had depended, pass from the world scene. Every evening, it was well known, King George would take up the telephone and speak to his sister, Princess Victoria. Together they would talk of the matters that affected them both, family matters and the memories they shared. The King would even open his mind and tell of the problems of State that confronted him, problems which only he could settle with the wisdom of his long statecraft. With the death of his sister, those evening talks and their consolation were denied him.

Above all, there was that matter of the heart. Not even the miracles of modern surgery can give a man a new heart. Millionaires or kings, paupers or labourers, all realise that the faint beating of their own hearts is the only life that is within them. What Nature gives, what storm and stress may wrack, all the fortune and power in the world cannot replace. And the heart of King George, which had survived so much, was in a weak state.

That previous illness, beginning in November 1928 as the result of a chill, had caused the greatest surgeons in the world much concern. It had necessitated two operations upon the King for the removal of fluid from the chest. The strain on the heart was tremendous. After a struggle, the King came through, but only the man himself and his intimates knew the effect that struggle had had upon his heart.

And now as the bitter winter of 1935–1936 prolonged itself the King began to feel the strain was too much. Even before he left Buckingham Palace for Sandringham, he expressed himself as feeling " very, very tired." It had been hoped that in the quiet of that Norfolk palace, bought by King Edward VII, his father, with its spacious lawns and flowering masses of rhododendron, a peaceful interlude in the increasing work of the State might be granted to him.

Christmas passed. Princes and princesses were gathered in a family party. Peace and goodwill had been proclaimed. The year 1936 had been ushered in auspiciously with every optimism. And then, on Friday, January 17, the King decided to remain in his bed. He was not feeling well. Lord Dawson of Penn and other famous surgeons were asked to be present at Sandringham.

Not until that evening did the British public realise that a drama of death had begun at the country palace in Norfolk. And even then, only a few tired listeners, yawning over their radio sets about midnight, suddenly heard an unexpected announcement.

" The following bulletin has been issued at Sandringham," came the unemotional voice of the announcer.

" The bronchial catarrh from which His Majesty the King is suffering is not severe ; but there have appeared signs of cardiac weakness which must be regarded with some disquiet. The bulletin is signed by Frederic Willans, Stanley Hewett, Dawson of Penn."

The next morning the newspapers displayed the news. Even then, it was not considered wise to treat it in alarmist fashion. It was further announced that during Friday night the King had slept peacefully.

But that broadcast bulletin came as a surprise to many. Even to men and women on the royal estate at Sandringham. On the Tuesday he had been seen by villagers walking on the Sandringham road, apparently in the best of health and spirits. " He looked as he always does," a village woman said to another after she had cleared away the breakfast table. " I curtsied to him, and the King wished me good-day in his usual kindly fashion. It came as a shock to all of us to learn how ill he was."

But already those famous doctors had taken their place by the bedside at Sandringham. They were Lord Dawson of Penn, who held the position of Physician-in-Ordinary to the King. It was Lord Dawson who attended His Majesty during his last serious illness in 1928. There was also Sir Stanley Hewett, Surgeon-Apothecary to the King since 1914, as also to the Prince of Wales, now King Edward VIII. Also Sir Frederic Willans, Surgeon-Apothecary to the King's Household since 1924. Finally, Sir Maurice Cassidy, a Physician-Extraordinary to His Majesty and a famous heart specialist.

Within a few hours these doctors had decided upon their diagnosis, and were taking instant action. The heart, always the heart, was the dominant factor in this illness. And it was upon the heart that they concentrated their attention.

The King was lying in a pleasant room on the first floor of the Sandringham home that he loved so well. His windows looked out to the west over a lovely vista of Norfolk heathland—typical of the county where he had spent so many of his happiest hours with his dogs and guns.

Members of the Royal Family were constantly at the bedside. The only ones who did not know were those grandchildren whom the King had shown his affection for in more than one public demonstration. Blissfully unconscious of the sorrow that had fallen upon the household, little Princess Elizabeth and Princess Margaret Rose romped in the snow in a nearby lane, laughingly bombarding a big snowman they had built.

Then the little Princesses were told: " Grandpapa is ill." It was decided to send them at once to London. They both put on their cherry-red coats and hats and, accompanied by the pet Welsh terrier " Yorkie," were driven to the station. That same evening they arrived at their London home.

No one in that household was more wracked with anxiety than Her Majesty, Queen Mary. Yet, in the true tradition of the Queen, she did not forget her duties to the people. Even while she was waiting anxiously for a decision by the doctors, she was penning the following telegram to send to the widow of another great friend of the King— Rudyard Kipling.

" The King and I are grieved to hear of the death this morning of Mr. Rud-

yard Kipling," wrote Queen Mary. " We shall mourn him, not only as a great national poet, but as a personal friend of many years. Please accept our heartfelt sympathy. . . ."

Then, putting down the pen, the Queen went back to that bedroom where King George to the world, but a real, devoted husband to herself, was fighting his last, losing battle against death.

The news vouchsafed by the doctors was anything but reassuring. Sir Maurice Cassidy had made a hurried departure, back to London. He was to obtain supplies of oxygen and enlist the services of three trained nurses. Among those nurses, inevitably, was the one who had shown again and again her devotion to the King—Sister Catherine Black, M.B.E., known as Nurse Black.

Everyone in the Royal Family knew this strongly built woman with the dark hair slightly greyed and the sympathetic dark blue eyes. Ever since the King's previous illness, Nurse Black had been a permanent member of the Royal Household Staff. Besides the King, she looked after any members of the Royal Family who might be indisposed. Her calm, low voice, so soothing in the sick room, her cool, efficient appearance, her discipline by the patient's bedside, had endeared her to all in the Royal Household. She was again at his bedside, accompanied by Nurse Davies, and later by Nurse Alcock. The supplies of oxygen were rushed by rail and road to Sandringham.

Sunday came, and for some hours it seemed that the doctors would triumph. But always the experts had to shake their head over the condition of the heart. They had issued late on Saturday night a further bulletin: " His Majesty the King has had some hours of restful sleep. The cardiac weakness and the embarrassment of the circulation have slightly increased and give cause for anxiety. . . ."

It all depended upon whether the King had now sufficient reserves of strength to fight through. The fact that he had reached the age of seventy, and for the five years since his previous illness had worked tremendously hard, was not in his favour. Still, the King was resting peacefully, and there was a chance.

II

At 7.45 p.m. on Sunday, a further bulletin was issued. "His Majesty the King has passed a quiet day," stated the doctors. "There is no change in His Majesty's condition." And throughout that fateful Sunday—which was to be the King's last clear day on earth—the patient upon whom the eyes of the world now centred slept peacefully for some hours.

But rumour and counter rumour had increased public anxiety. In London, despite the bitterly cold wet weather, the pavements by Buckingham Palace were thronged all day and late into the night by vast crowds eagerly awaiting news of the King's progress. As each bulletin was posted, there was a surge forward by those rain-drenched crowds.

In Sandringham itself, where life seemed to have gone on tiptoe, there was a comforting sense of warmth and hope. The sun shone brilliantly. In sheltered places the crisp and sparkling snow slowly bared patches of herbage for the King's deer. In Sandringham Church, that Sunday morning, there gathered many of the King's oldest and most devoted friends, men and women who

had lived and worked on the estate through all the years the King has reigned and longer.

No member of the Royal Family could attend that little, homely service. But, as the congregation rose with a quiet shuffle of feet at the entrance of the minister, all eyes turned instinctively to the pew where but a week ago the King had kneeled in prayer.

From the pulpit the rector, the Rev. Arthur Fuller, speaking in tones that betrayed the profound emotion he shared with his little flock, sought to give courage and comfort to troubled hearts and minds. He said:

" I am authorised to say that His Majesty the King has increased in strength since yesterday."

A sigh of thankfulness answered him.

Then, taking a text from St. Peter's exhortation: " Casting all your care upon Him . . ." the rector spoke of the power of faith and prayer in this time of great anxiety.

He finally quoted these words, spoken by the Archbishop of Canterbury in Canterbury Cathedral the previous day:

" I am sure that the love and loyalty which were so wonderfully manifested in the King's Jubilee Year will be expressed now by the prayers of all his people that the Holy Spirit, the Lord and Giver of Life, may bring to him full strength and recovery; may give trust and confidence to the Queen, and may give wisdom and skill to those who have care of him.

" Let us all pray that a life which means so much to this realm may be restored to full health and strength."

The usual prayers for the King and members of the Royal Family were offered, and the rector's voice trembled as he added special prayers for the

IN HIS LAST CHRISTMAS-DAY BROADCAST, *speaking from Sandringham, King George said, "It is this personal link between me and my people which I value more than I can say. It binds us together in all our common joys and sorrows."*

THE LAST PHOTOGRAPH *ever taken of King George, as he was leaving London to spend Christmas at Sandringham. Soon afterwards, his fatal illness occurred.*

FOUR PICTURES OF PRINCE GEORGE *when he was a small boy. With him in one photograph are his father and eldest brother, the Duke of Clarence.*

THE FIRST TWO PHOTOGRAPHS SHOW PRINCE GEORGE *and the Duke of Clarence when they were naval cadets. The lower photograph shows him with his brother and sisters, the late Princess Royal, Queen Maud of Norway, and Princess Victoria.*

HIS NICKNAME OF "THE SAILOR KING" was well merited, for he loved the Navy and was always at his happiest when he was visiting it. This war-time photograph shows him mounting a ladder from a submarine.

King's recovery and that prayer from the Order for the Visitation of the Sick: " Hear us, Almighty and Most Merciful God and Saviour; extend Thy accustomed goodness to this Thy servant who is grieved with sickness."

But in the meantime, the business of statecraft had been seriously interrupted by this sudden illness of the King. It was decided, as in the previous illness of the King, that a Council of State should be formed to act for the King. This practice of appointing a Council of State to carry out certain duties of the Sovereign during his illness or absence abroad dates back to Norman times.

In modern usage, such a Council possesses all the powers necessary for carrying on the administration of the Government in the King's name—with certain exceptions that include the conferment of honours and the summoning or dissolving of Parliament.

The signatures of at least three Counsellors of State are necessary for a document which would normally require the assent of the King alone.

During the twenty-five years of the King's reign only three such Councils had been appointed. The last was in 1928, during the King's grave illness. The Council of State on that occasion comprised the Queen, the Prince of Wales, the Duke of York, the Archbishop of Canterbury, the Lord Chancellor, and the Prime Minister. It was appointed at perhaps one of the most remarkable meetings of the Privy Council ever held. It was held in the Audience Chamber next to the King's bedroom, the door leading into the bedroom being open. The Home Secretary, then Sir William Joynson-Hicks, stood in the doorway and read the Order

Paper so that the King, in bed a few feet away, could be fully cognisant of the proceedings. His Majesty then signed the document with his own hand.

Once again, therefore, it was decided to call together the Privy Council for the election of a Council of State. Telegrams were sent off from Sandringham summoning the Home Secretary, Sir John Simon, Mr. Ramsay MacDonald, Lord President of the Council, Viscount Hailsham, Lord Chancellor, and Sir Maurice Hankey, Clerk of the Council.

At the same time the Prince of Wales motored from Sandringham during the morning accompanied by the Duke of York. There was a double anxiety for the Duke of York. He intended to go at once to the Royal Lodge, Great Windsor Park, where the Duchess was recovering from a severe attack of influenzal pneumonia.

After leaving his brother at the Royal Lodge, the Prince of Wales went on to London. There he proceeded straight to Downing Street, where he was able to give the Prime Minister, Mr. Stanley Baldwin, the latest news of the King's condition. Mr. Baldwin had decided, in view of the serious state of affairs, to remain in London during the week-end. There, in the historic Number 10, the details of continuing work of the State were soon settled.

The Prince of Wales, after spending forty minutes with Mr. Baldwin, then went by car to Buckingham Palace. Later he proceeded to his brother's quarters at York House, St. James's Palace. There he made special arrangements so that both he and the Duke of York could be in immediate telephonic communication with Sandringham during the night that would be spent in London.

III

Monday, January 20, the fateful day came. In the early hours of the morning, little groups of people, despite the severe weather, were still to be found outside the wet, beaded railings of Buckingham Palace. Earlier in the evening three small children—two girls and a boy—walked past, and the tallest stood on tip-toes to read the notice to the other two. Then, standing back a few paces, all three of them solemnly sang the first verse of the National Anthem.

At the same time the world-wide concern was to be seen in the sheaf of telegrams and radio messages that descended upon that country palace in Norfolk. Herr Hitler of Germany was among the first to dispatch a message. " I have just learned of Your Majesty's serious illness," he telegraphed. " I wish on this occasion to express my most sincere and heartiest wishes for a speedy convalescence and a complete recovery." Newspapers on the Continent, in the United States, in South America, and in far-off foreign states displayed their concern at this sudden illness. The Monday that was ushered in was a black Monday. Gloom settled all over the world. It was realised that one of the greatest forces for peace was in danger in that Norfolk countryside.

The morning opened at Sandringham with the arrival of Cabinet Ministers by motor-car from London. These cars entered the wide gravel drives leading to the house, and the oppressive silence of the countryside and the static groups of villagers told in simple fashion of a tense waiting that was reflected throughout the whole wide world where King George was known and revered.

The Lord President of the Council, Mr. Ramsay MacDonald, the Lord Chancellor, Lord Hailsham, the Home Secretary, Sir John Simon, and the Clerk to the Council, Sir Maurice Hankey, arrived by special train. They then motored to the house, where they were received by Lord Wigram, the King's private secretary. They were at once conducted into the presence of the Queen.

Then followed the quiet but intensely dramatic scene culminating in the appointment of the Queen and her four sons as Counsellors of State, investing them with the powers of the Sovereign.

Mr. MacDonald and his colleagues sat at a table in the King's dressing-room, which was between his bedroom and the Queen's. The communicating doors between the dressing-room and the King's bedroom were opened wide, and the Privy Councillors could see where the King lay, his head raised on his pillows.

The document authorising the temporary transfer of the Sovereign powers had been already drawn up and nothing was needed but the King's signature.

Two authoritative descriptions of that poignant scene have been given to us.

" At noon of that day," said Dr. Lang, Archbishop of Canterbury, " the King, propped up in his chair, looking so frail and weak, received his last Privy Council. To the order constituting a Council of State he gave in his old clear tones the familiar ' Approved.' Then he made deliberate and repeated efforts, most gallant but most pathetic, to sign his last State paper with his own hand.

Then, when the effort was too great for him, he turned to his Council with a last kindly and kingly smile.

" It was a scene which those who beheld it will never forget. I hope I have been guilty of no impropriety in describing it. I think it is worthy of record. It shows that what rallied him to his last conscious hours was this old and undeviating response to the claims of duty. . . ."

And here is Sir John Simon, present in his capacity as Home Secretary :

" After a pause, during which the King was making those gallant but pathetic efforts to sign his name, he turned to the Councillors present and said, quietly and simply : 'I am so sorry to keep you waiting like this.' Those were the last words we heard him utter. As we withdrew, he turned and gave to each of us a kindly little smile and nod with which he was accustomed to end an audience."

Finally, with low bows and quiet expression of their heartfelt hope for the King's recovery, the Privy Council dismissed itself.

After luncheon with the Queen, Mr. MacDonald and his colleagues prepared to return to London. By this time the Prince of Wales, with the Duke of York, had flown back from London in his private aeroplane and landed at the R.A.F. station at Bircham Newton, eight miles from Sandringham.

The machine had flown over Sandringham on its way to the landing-ground, and the Queen—as was her usual habit whenever the Prince was flying in the vicinity—kept watch for his coming. Ordinarily, the Prince would circle Sandringham House, but on this day, to avoid disturbing the King with the noise of the engine, he omitted this.

Mr. MacDonald, Lord Hailsham, and Sir John Simon accepted the invitation of the Prince to use his aeroplane for their return to London.

In the meantime, the Duchess of Kent had arrived by train. Unaccompanied, except for members of the Duke's suite, she was met at Wolferton Station by one of the Royal motor-cars. She arrived at Sandringham just in time to join the other members of the Royal Family for a walk in the grounds.

With the Prince of Wales on her right, the Queen walked briskly through the grounds. The Duke of Gloucester, who had been suffering from a throat affection, was unable to be present at Sandringham. For the moment his doctors had deemed it inadvisable for him to travel.

And so the afternoon passed on. Anxiously the Royal Family awaited the verdict of the doctors who were conducting another examination of the patient.

The doctors came forth. One glance at their faces revealed their concern. They had found that there had been a sharp change for the worse. They decided to issue a serious bulletin. It appeared at 5.30 in the afternoon.

" The condition of His Majesty the King shows diminishing strength," it was stated.

The news created dismay. It meant that, although no change in the King's condition had been detected, he had been all the time, slowly but imperceptibly, losing strength, and his heart had been slowly growing weaker.

Steadily he grew worse. It was now that the voice of the announcer of the B.B.C began to tell the world and the millions of listeners of the final, desperate fight of the King against death. Those broadcast announcements, when all other programmes were ceased, remain in the minds of those who heard them as the most poignant and dramatic utterances through the microphone.

At 9.25 p.m. it became apparent that the King was dying. The doctors issued that final bulletin. In a voice of quiet sympathy, Chief Announcer Hibberd gave the bulletin to the waiting nation :

" The King's life is moving peacefully towards its close."

So the King lost his gallant fight. His slow weakening was described as " a general slowing up of the bodily machine."

Then the B.B.C. stations closed down until 10 p.m. Later, the striking of Big Ben was broadcast, and the 9.25 bulletin was read again.

A brief interlude of prayer was then announced : " We invite you to join in recollection and prayer for our King." And a choir sang, " Whosoever shall endure unto the end, he shall be saved," followed by the 23rd Psalm.

This was followed by the Lord's Prayer.

Listeners awaiting a further announcement, for a time heard nothing but the fateful ticking of a clock.

All the evening there was a stillness in the red-carpeted room at Sandringham where the King lay. All lights were turned off. The only light was that given by a fire of logs.

The Queen sat at the King's side, her hand in his. Since five o'clock she had not left him. She waited. The King was not able to speak to her.

But at nine o'clock he was still conscious. He looked up to his wife. Their eyes met. The Queen did not speak.

Slowly the King's breathing became more and more laboured. His doctors and his nurses stood close to him. They could do no more.

The Prince of Wales waited in an adjoining room with his sister, the Princess Royal, his brothers, the Duke of York and the Duke of Kent, and his sister-in-law, the Duchess of Kent. All were silent.

Dinner was prepared. It passed unserved. The Princess Royal was weeping. The Duchess of Kent sought to comfort her. The Archbishop of Canterbury, an old and intimate friend of the Royal Family, remained in the King's bedroom. He prayed.

All the time, the Queen sat by her husband, unweeping, motionless, refusing to leave his side. The minutes passed while the King hovered between life and death. As his life ebbed, more oxygen was given to him to relieve his breathing. Injections were given to aid his flagging heart. For a short time the King was delirious, calling out many times the name of the grey pony, Jock, he loved so well.

Soon it became apparent that the end was imminent. Silently, the Royal Family gathered around the bed of the dying King. In that last hour he sank into a coma. He spoke no word. And, peacefully, he died. The hour was the same as that at which his father, King Edward, died in 1910.

The Queen leaned over him, kissed

AN INTERESTING INFORMAL PHOTOGRAPH *of Prince George and Princess Mary, taken soon after their marriage.*

A FAMILY GROUP *with his wife, his mother, and his children.*

PRINCE GEORGE, in Highland dress, shown drilling his young son, now the Duke of Gloucester. Appropriately enough, his third son was the only one to adopt an Army career.

WITH HIS ELDEST SON, *after one of his tours abroad.   King George was the most-travelled monarch Britain had ever had, and he encouraged his sons to seek knowledge and experience by visiting all parts of the world.*

THE KING *was always an enthusiastic devotee of yachting. Here is an unusual picture of him aboard his yacht* Britannia *during some rough weather.*

his brow, and then, with the arms of the Prince of Wales around her, she was led from the room. She was in tears.

In the passage outside the Queen turned to her son, the new King. Mother and son embraced affectionately. The new King was greatly moved. His sister, the Princess Royal, collapsed and had to be assisted to her room.

Down the darkened drive from Sandringham House, a bareheaded youth came riding a cycle with a dim oil-lamp flickering in front of it. In an old brown leather case, which he carried in one hand, while the other gripped the handlebars, he brought the news of the death of King George.

The youth rode swiftly and without dismounting, without even stopping he delivered the fateful message at the lodge gate. A silent group of villagers had been standing there for hours. They read the news. There was a suspicion of a sob, and quietly they dispersed.

But, as the news spread, they were replaced by other people. They came in sorrowing crowds about the gates of the house, the men scarce able to repress their tears, the women crying. In the darkness they moved in dim, uncertain crowds, for ever looking towards the house where their beloved King had gone to his end.

At 12.15 a.m. in London, Sir John Reith's quiet voice told all parts of the Empire that the King was dead.

"This is London," he said. "It is with great sorrow that we make the following announcement. His Majesty the King passed peacefully away at a few minutes before twelve. He whom we loved as King has passed from our midst. We voice the grief of all the peoples of his Empire.

"We offer profound sympathy to Her Majesty the Queen and to the Royal Family. With our fellow-citizens at home and overseas, we affirm our loyalty to the Crown. . . ."

London itself had been stilled ever since that fateful bulletin earlier in the evening. Hotels, clubs, and restaurants stopped all music, soon after ten o'clock, as soon as the gravity of the King's condition became known. There were few people at theatres or cinemas. Most had stayed at home to listen to the radio news.

In Downing Street were three policemen and a little knot of people watching the lighted windows of No. 10, behind the drawn blinds of which Mr. and Mrs. Baldwin awaited with the nation the grave news.

At twenty minutes past twelve an official walked across from Buckingham Palace towards the railings where the earlier bulletins had been posted. The crowd, still standing there, watched his approach in complete silence. As he reached the railings he said in a quiet voice to those within hearing : "The King passed away at a few minutes to twelve."

Those who had heard the message passed the tragic news to those behind them. Every man bared his head. There was no movement for several minutes. The throng seemed stunned. The silence was broken only by the rhythmic tramp, tramp, tramp of the sentries marching up and down. Not even the King's death could cease their vigil.

The news of the King's death was flashed around the world in a few seconds. From Sandringham House it was sent to the India Office, the Dominions Office, and the Foreign

Office, to be sent from them all over the globe. Telephone, telegraph, and radio carried the messages. The Admiralty wirelessed direct to all His Majesty's ships at sea. Intimation of the death was communicated to Windsor Castle by the private wire from Sandringham, and the royal flagman lowered the Union Jack to half-mast.

Within a few minutes of the official bulletin being issued, the silence that had fallen over Sandringham House was broken by the roar of a powerful car which sped through the night out of the royal gates towards the London Road. It bore Lord Wigram, King George's secretary, on his way to see the Prime Minister in London.

Immediately the death was announced, the Queen herself spoke over the telephone to members of the Royal Family who were not at Sandringham. The Duke and Duchess of Gloucester at Buckingham Palace, the Duchess of York at Windsor, the Duke of Connaught at Bath, and Queen Maud of Norway at Oslo—the only surviving child of King Edward and Queen Alexandra—were all informed.

The new King sent the following telegram to the Lord Mayor of London, Sir Percy Vincent :

" I am deeply grieved to inform you that my beloved father the King passed away peacefully at 11.55 p.m.
" (Signed) Edward."

It was the first time the signature " Edward " had been used. Hitherto the signature had been " Edward P."

Shortly after his father died the Prince of Wales was summoned to meet the members of the Privy Council present at Sandringham House. The Prince spoke to his brothers in low tones. The Prince became King of England without any ceremony. He was addressed a few moments later by the Archbishop of Canterbury as " Your Majesty."

Then the Archbishop knelt and led the family in prayers.

IV

And so died His Most Excellent Majesty George the Fifth by the Grace of God of Great Britain, Ireland, and of the British Dominions beyond the Seas, King, Defender of the Faith, Emperor of India.

It remained for the Prime Minister of Great Britain to speak the nation's tribute to a great monarch in a message broadcast the following evening. Speaking with obvious emotion, Mr. Stanley Baldwin said :

" ' After he had served his own generation by the will of God, he fell on sleep and was laid unto his fathers.'

" Those words kept recurring to me in the watches of last night, for if there was one thing that our King had done, it was to serve his own generation by the will of God, and because of that the news of the death of His Majesty, when it came, has been heard everywhere with a personal grief, not only in this country but through the vast Empire over which he bore rule and, I believe, far beyond its borders.

" To famous men all the earth is a sepulchre. It is less than a month ago that the voice now silent was heard around the world, a King addressing his subjects, a father seated with his family speaking to his people, members of his wider family, words of wisdom, courage, and deep human sympathy. And it is as members of a family that we are mourning him to-day. There must be millions who feel as I do that a wise and loving friend and counsellor has been taken from us, and for long the world will seem a poorer and colder place without him, and the tones of that well-known voice are echoing in our ears to-day as our thoughts turn to the widowed Queen and to the bereaved family.

"And I do want to say a word to you about Queen Mary, for I know that every heart in the Empire is sore for her this night. It often seems to me that in a married life so perfect, so happy as theirs was, there has to come that inevitable day when one is taken and the other is left, and one of the two has to continue the pilgrimage to the end alone. There are millions of hands which, if they could reach the Queen, would be stretched out to her, and tears of sympathy would be shed with her, and it must be some comfort to her, though we cannot tell her that, to know of that feeling, and she must know it from the events of that wonderful Jubilee summer; but may not this be a comfort to her as it has been a comfort to others, that, after all, the one who is left is really carrying the cross for the one who has gone before?

"If she were not suffering to-day, he would be, and she is bearing what might have been his sorrow for him : and I cannot help feeling that with a King, knowing how lonely the high places of the world are, and knowing that he has no one but his wife with whom he might have really intimate converse— I tremble to think what it might have been for him had he been alone in his awful task with no voice by him to cheer, to comfort, and to encourage.

We are thankful, indeed, to feel that even in her sorrow Queen Mary is spared to the people who love her, and I am sure that we all of us, all our people, will show her in whatever way they can how close she is to their hearts, and how they will treasure her not only for the King's sake but for her own.

"And as to the King, what can I say in a few minutes and within twenty-four hours of this shattering blow? I think I may dwell for these few minutes on the King as I have known him during this last year, and try to picture him as one who has borne the responsibilities of his position during perhaps the most difficult quarter of a century in which a monarch has ever sat on our Throne. There was no respite for him during those twenty-five years. The whole world has been in a state of commotion, and there never seemed to come to him any period when he could look ahead for two or three years and feel that all would be peace and quiet and nothing in the world to cause him or his people trouble. The world has been what a great man of the sixteenth century called it, ' a raving world,' and he played his part in it gallantly to the end, and I do feel most thankful that after that illness of his six years ago he was spared to see that Jubilee year.

"He and his Ministers and his doctors and, I think, all who knew much about these things felt some apprehension as to the strain he might have to undergo in attending the various ceremonies and functions that belonged to that time. But all our fears were belied, for there seemed to be given to him a special strength to go through those weeks. And I rejoice that he, modest as ever, diffident as to his own powers, often wondering what his people thought of what he had done and tried to do for them—I often think that it was a most wonderful experience for him to see, to have brought home to him, that all he had done had sunk deep into their hearts. The occasion of that Jubilee was the occasion that they all embraced to throw off that shyness so characteristic of us, and show him openly and without shame that they were proud of him as their King, that they loved him as a man.

"The effect on him, I think, was great. He never referred to it without emotion. He was touched profoundly. He accepted that tribute with a thankful humility. I am indeed thankful that he lived to see it, and that during the last months he knew what he meant to his people. But we knew that there was no strength to spare. To go through that last illness had taken from him every reserve of strength that he had. We knew that it must go hard with him if any illness should attack him, even were it a slight one, and I myself noticed in the months that followed the Jubilee—and I have never known him so gentle, so calm—an increase even of his customary kindliness, and I had a feeling, which I expressed to my friends through all the autumn, that he was ready for the long journey that he was so soon to take.

"He was tired at times, and I used to contrast his lot with the lot of the politicians, for we can and do have our old age, if we live, to ourselves. But the King's burden is never lifted. It goes on all through the year, and it goes on with age, and the only release from it is death. And then, again, you will remember the death of his sister. Many who are listening to me to-night may be elderly brothers and sisters, perhaps between sixty and seventy years of age. You know what a link that is, the common memories of childhood, and there are few losses as men and women get older, few losses that strike so deep as those of contemporary relations with their share of common memories. And it was no ordinary bond, no formal bond, that united the King and his sister. They were devoted to each other, and His Majesty, if he had not seen her, would talk to her on the telephone every night and tell her what he had been doing to cheer her and make her life less lonely. I think that he felt the severance of that old tie very keenly.

"I saw him for the last time when we parted for the Christmas holidays. It is the only time in the year that I am able to go to my own home, and he was going to his at Sandringham, and we were rejoicing together, for we both loved the same kind of holiday, and we were going to spend it with our own children and with our grandchildren at our own home in the country. It was but a few days after that when the first intimation reached us that all was not well. At the end of last week and during the week-end I was in constant touch with Sandringham, and it was only yesterday morning the King's Secretary rang me up to tell me that he had seen a change, and that he feared that the end could not be long delayed.

"There is one thing I think I can tell you without any impropriety, for though much, and most indeed, of what passes near the end is sacred, and we none of us have the desire or right to inquire into what happened at those times, yet I think I may tell you this. The King was having brief intervals of consciousness, and each time he became conscious it was some kind inquiry or kind observation of someone, some words of gratitude for kindness shown. But he did say to his secretary when he sent for him : ' How is the Empire ? ' An unusual phrase in that form, and the secretary said : ' All is well, sir, with the Empire,' and the King gave him a smile and relapsed once more into unconsciousness.

" It was simply this, that during all that time subconsciously and just coming to the surface at odd moments was that same love for his people, care for their well-being here and throughout the world, for that family to whom he spoke last Christmas, and the thought of them was with him to the end. King George, it is true, inherited his position on the Throne, but he won his own way to the hearts of his people. Behind the pomp and the pageantry incidental to his great position he laboured night and day in that high station to which God had called him. The doing of his duty to the utmost of his ability was the guiding principle of his life.

" Great power which corrupts weak natures ennobled our King's character and made him subdue passion and will and energy to his duty to his country. He brought the dispositions that are lovely in private life into the service and conduct of the Commonwealth, and not only in virtue of his office but in virtue of his person was he the first gentleman in the land. As the knowledge of the King's complete dedication to duty grew and spread as his reign proceeded, so did the respect of his people turn into reverence and reverence into love. It is literally true that he won their hearts, and during the Jubilee they made that manifest to him.

" This is the truth we must bear in mind as we think of the son who succeeds to the Throne and upon whom has now fallen one of the heaviest burdens that can rest upon the shoulders of fallible and mortal man. We can best honour the noble memory of King George by gathering round and sustaining the young King who for so long we have delighted to know as the Prince of Wales. All eyes are upon him as he advances to his father's place, and, while he is no stranger to public duty, he is now summoned to face responsibilities more onerous, more exacting, more continuous, than any he has hitherto been asked to discharge.

" He comes to them in the prime of his powers, and already known throughout the length and breadth of his Empire. His great gifts of mind and heart he is now called upon to consecrate to his people. He inherits an example of kingly conduct, of virtue, of wisdom, and of endurance. King George's reign was marked by far-reaching constitutional and Parliamentary changes without precedent in our long history. He earned the loyalty and respect of all parties in the State, new and old. He hands down in turn to his son the throne he himself received from his father, and he hands it down with its foundations strengthened, its moral authority, its honour, and its dignity enhanced. It is an incomparable and awe-inspiring inheritance.

" The young King knows the confidence we all repose in him. He knows that he commands not only the allegiance, he knows that the understanding, the affection, and the prayers of the countless multitudes of his subjects are with him at this hour. May God guide him aright, and God Save the King."

CHAPTER II

BIRTH AND EDUCATION

King George's Strength of Character—His birth on June 3, 1865—"Healthy naughtiness"—Off to sea—A world tour aboard the Bacchante—*Promotion in the Navy—Death of Duke of Clarence—His betrothal and marriage to Princess Mary.*

I

"ENGLISH history is dignified, but unexciting." So comments more than one Continental critic, slightly dishevelled from the melodramatic hurly-burly of history on the other side of the English Channel.

Yet English history now in the making can be said to be not only exciting, but the most significant in the human world of to-day.

When at five minutes to midnight on January 20, 1936, in the country quiet of Sandringham, King George V breathed his last, there came to an end what was undoubtedly the most dramatic as well as the greatest epoch in the history of England.

For twenty-five years—a quarter of a century—a slight bearded man with a kindly smile had been at the head of the greatest confederation of self-governing states that the world has ever known. Through the modern miracle of broadcasting, the strong but feeling voice of this Emperor was known to the humblest of his subjects. Daily in the panoply of royalty or as an ordinary citizen, he had appeared before his people. No task was too great, no function too dull, no undertaking too arduous for this slightly built man acclaimed as King George. And because he was never surrounded by armed forces, except for ceremonial purposes, or shadowed by guards fearing assassination, he was in every sense a King of the people. Yet, in his person he represented a kingship more powerful than that enjoyed by the Oriental despots or Roman Cæsars of history. His territories were wider and more populous than those of the Great Moghul or Jenghis Khan. Even the Holy Empire of Spain in its zenith could not equal the wealth and spaciousness of these world states ruled by George V. The kings and rulers of states to-day who walked reverently behind the gun-carriage that trundled through the streets of London carrying the mortal remains of this Emperor, truly envied the majesty and security of King George V during his reign.

Mighty as that Empire was, however, it was founded on a real basis of democracy and self-government. It had developed into a confederation of states acknowledged to be the greatest force for peace in a world still cursed by the itch for war. And each State in this confederation recognised the kingship of George V as the real, binding force.

It is the fashion of to-day to declare that the moment produces the man. A crisis may arise, but also the individual capable of grappling with it. When the historians of the future

THE PRINCES' LIFE aboard the Britannia was a busy one. Their tutor was also in the ship, and they studied for six hours a day. Apart from this, they were treated in the same way as other cadets. Prince George received the nickname "Sprat" because of his size.

WHEN PRINCE GEORGE *was twelve, he and his elder brother, the Duke of Clarence, joined the Navy as cadets aboard the Britannia. This photograph was taken during their two years' apprenticeship.*

attempt to analyse the bewildering chaos of the world in the twentieth century they will acclaim not only the statesmen and that peculiar genius for sane government which is the English heritage; they will point to the symbol of that Government, the King, and maybe marvel that a man dare shoulder such responsibilities, dare endure and toil throughout a lifetime to ensure that the confederation of states and the overwhelming desire for peace in the world should prevail. No ordinary man standing on the threshold of the twentieth century and realising instinctively the tremendous forces that were about to be loosed, could have stepped on to the throne of England without a shiver. George V stepped forward boldly and without hesitation. He accepted the duties and responsibilities of his position. He had to be the man of the moment. And by his years of unswerving devotion to those duties, he assumes a place in world history to an extent that cannot be gauged by the writer of to-day.

That confederation of world states, known loosely as the British Empire, is his finest monument. It was, in a sense, a reflection of his own tactful, generous, and compromising personality. Millions of different coloured people—white, brown, black, and yellow—recognised in that slight, bearded figure the symbol of their hopes and ambitions. In a world that had been shattered by wars and revolutions, where thrones had been overturned and dictators risen from the ranks, where brute force had triumphed and the streets of civilised cities seen gutters run red, those peoples who proudly acknowledged George V as their ruler had achieved the reality of that prayer in all English churches—" peace in our time."

But this peace of the Commonwealth of Nations had not been achieved without a struggle. It had suffered its agonies, its bloody moments. There was the period within living memory when the world waited breathlessly for what seemed the inevitable collapse, the resounding downfall of this Empire ruled by King George V. The terrible losses and sufferings of the Great War had been followed by the financial and economic losses of the Great Slump. Money crashes in the City of London. British shipping idle. Millions of unemployed mounting. Hunger marches. Heavy and crippling taxation. Fierce economies in the Navy, Army, and Air Force. Britain abandoned the gold standard. The City of London was no longer the money mart of the world. The Commonwealth of Nations seemed to be ebbing of its life blood. The whole structure seemed to be cracking.

At such a time, the world gazed at that symbol—King George V. No man in those terrible times must have felt so dreadfully alone, so pathetically human in the face of inhuman forces, as did the tired and ageing man seated at his desk in Buckingham Palace. Those anxious days took their toll on the King's health. Remorselessly, the wheels of state ground on, and only the slavish devotion to duty and the unending preoccupation with State affairs by the King himself kept the great Commonwealth of Nations from that collapse for which the world waited. Ministers came and departed. New ministers and more ministers. Men with ideas and men without ideas. Crude policies and nostrums. The only man who remained was the one with the greatest knowledge of state-craft of them all—King George V.

For him there was no resignation. No rest in a country house with dogs and books. No abandonment of the hurly-burly of day-to-day statecraft for the slightly cynical philosophy of the man who escapes. No time to rum-mage among past State documents and write a history of contemporary events with oneself as the dramatic hero. These pleasures of the retired or dis-missed statesman were not for the age-ing and tired man in Buckingham Palace.

He rose each day to a pile of new problems, a crop of new despairs. And he faced them with a courage and stead-fastness in those dark times which made the ordinary politician marvel.

There came a realisation by those ordinary politicians that they had never really known, never truly estimated this man at the helm of affairs who was staunch in his belief that the Empire would win through. The ordinary petty potentate would have seized the opportunity to let loose the reins of State, leave the country to its chaos and end his own days in peaceful epicurean-ism somewhere between Monte Carlo and Nice. No such idea was ever entertained for one moment by King George.

And those years of endurance had their reward. As the year of the Jubilee came, King George from his throne could gaze upon a Britain and an Empire greater, more free and, above all, mightier than it had ever been.

The miracle had been achieved. Once again London was the money mart of the world. Strife and dissen-sion had ceased, and the Empire had settled down securely in its apparently loose constitutional form, and yet bound more firmly than ever to the King-Emperor himself. The falling graph of economics had taken the upward trend. Employment was increasing. There was every indication that a new and greater prosperity lay ahead. And in those Jubilee celebrations the people vouchsafed their own thanks and loyalty to the man who had remained at the head of affairs through all the storm and stress.

That statesman with the true world vision, General Smuts, summed up the situation in a fine panegyric:

" If the King had passed away five years ago, when his life was literally snatched from death," said General Smuts, " the rich drama of his reign would have been in a sense incom-plete.

" He was aware of the affection and gratitude of his people, but being a modest, humble man, he could have had no conception of the depth of their devotion to him personally. That realisation came at the Jubilee—a greater triumph than ever a Roman Emperor enjoyed after a mighty victory. He stood out as the most beloved figure among the rulers of the world. The drama was at last complete. . . ."

Looking round upon the great vic-tory of Peace that he had won for Britain and the Empire, King George could rightly consider that his task was now ended. He had passed with the country through the dark valley of despair and dissension. The sunshine was now visible again. He could rightly rest from his long and weary labours.

And so, with a sigh, he came to the peaceful end.

PRINCE GEORGE *with his elder brother and Princess Charlotte of Saxe-Coburg-Gotha.*

ANOTHER STUDY of *Prince George with his father, then Prince of Wales, and his brother the Duke of Clarence.*

PRINCE GEORGE *photographed on board his father's yacht with his sisters.*

PRINCE GEORGE *at the age of twenty-one. He had just been promoted to lieutenant, and later in the year was appointed to H.M.S.* Thunderer.

PRINCE GEORGE *aboard a destroyer which he commanded during manœuvres.*

PRINCE GEORGE *with the Duke of Edinburgh at Malta.*

II

The birth of the boy who was to become King George V caused no very great excitement in Britain on that day, June 3, 1865, when it was announced in the papers. Only among those who formed the Society that circled about the Court of Queen Victoria was there considerable surprise. And perhaps that surprise was justified.

The previous evening, the Prince and Princess of Wales were giving an important dinner-party at Marlborough House. The bluff, hospitable Prince, later to become King Edward VII, received his important guests alone, apologising for the absence of the Princess of Wales by saying that she had been present at an afternoon concert and was somewhat fatigued.

But besides the important statesmen, there were also wives and several lovely ladies. The band of the Scots Guards was playing, there was a good deal of talk and laughter, and the chandeliers glittered down upon a bejewelled throng reflecting the brilliance. Altogether, it was a joyous, festive evening, and the guests thoroughly enjoyed themselves—as they invariably did at Marlborough House. It was nearing midnight before the gay throng dispersed, making their bows to the Prince of Wales.

Then, as those same guests rose the next morning to take their tea and toast and unfold the morning paper, it was to read the official news that Her Royal Highness the Princess of Wales had been safely delivered of a son at 1.18 a.m. and that both the Princess and infant were perfectly well.

The event, of course, was not entirely unexpected, but was at least before time. This second son of the Prince and Princess of Wales caused, at his birth, the grandmother Queen Victoria to dip pen into ink and write another of those wise and now famous letters.

On this occasion, Queen Victoria wrote to the King of the Belgians. She pointed out that whereas the elder brother had made his appearance two months before he was expected, " Alix was again confined too soon, but this time only a month, and the child is said to be nice and plump and much larger than Albert Victor."

Perhaps it was only natural that there should not have been the same excitement over this birth as there was on the occasion of the previous son, later to be known as the Duke of Clarence. For the elder brother was marked out for the Throne. This younger son would, on reaching manhood, be required only to share the many onerous public duties performed by the Royal Family.

Nevertheless, in an almost matriarch spirit, Queen Victoria was soon concerning herself over the baptism and the future names of this grandson. She obviously disliked the name " George " when it was first suggested. The Prince of Wales pointed out to his mother that " George " was the name of the Patron Saint of England and, clinching the argument further, mentioned that the Duke of Cambridge was, in reality, " Uncle George."

The Queen at last gave way, but in giving her consent she also wrote to Edward from Balmoral : " Of course you will add ' Albert ' at the end, like your brothers, as you know we settled long ago that all dearest Papa's male descendants should bear that name."

ON JULY 6TH, 1893, *he married Princess Mary, daughter of the Duchess of Teck. Following the death of his brother in the previous year, he came into direct line of succession to the Throne and was created Duke of York.*

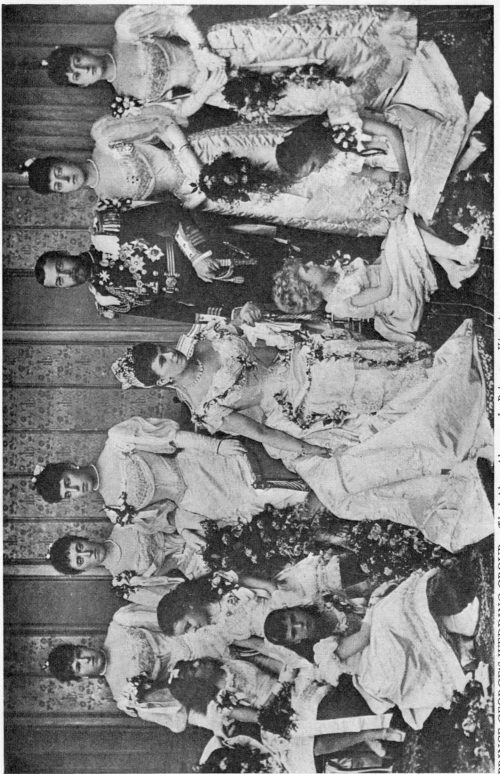

PRINCE GEORGE'S WEDDING GROUP. *The bridesmaids were the Princesses Victoria and Maud of Wales, and Princesses Victoria of Edinburgh, Alexandra of Edinburgh, Beatrice of Edinburgh, Victoria Louise of Schleswig-Holstein, Margaret of Connaught, Patricia of Connaught, Victoria Eugénie of Battenberg, and Victoria Alice of Battenberg.*

And so, on July 8, in the Private Chapel at Windsor, in the presence of the Royal Family and many distinguished foreign representatives, the Archbishop of Canterbury took the child in his arms and solemnly baptised him " George Frederick Ernest Albert."

For the occasion, the Prince Consort had himself composed an anthem. The choir sang it in the chapel.

In life's gay morn, ere sprightly youth
By vice and folly is enslaved . . .

Thus the future King George V entered upon the royal scene.

III

As to how princes should be educated, Machiavelli has written a shrewd treatise. For the sons of the heir to the British Throne, however, a really democratic and human form of education had to be devised. Very early, Edward and Alexandra concerned themselves with this important factor, as also did Queen Victoria. With much care a tutor was selected for the two young Princes.

John Neale Dalton was the man chosen, and to him King George in his later years could look back with affection and a debt of gratitude. The tutor soon endeared himself to all in the Royal Family. Even Queen Victoria could write of him : " Mr. Dalton has the children's interests most closely at heart."

The two young princes discovered that their tutor was no mere book crammer, no purveyor of dry-as-dust knowledge. In fact, he had a habit of closing books early in the day and

taking his two young charges on visits to galleries and museums, historical sights, and monuments. Generally speaking, the training of the two young princes proceeded together and was of that rigorous character which prevailed in the Victorian age.

There are engaging incidents on record to give us a picture of Prince George as a boy. Mr. Hector Bolitho in his book *Victoria, The Widow and Her Son*, gives us a glimpse of the 'sixties and 'seventies when the two young princes were growing boys.

Prince George was brought up in awe of his father, whose genial nature never lessened his sense of princely right. But the authority which Edward exercised over his sons was never relentless nor unsympathetic. The healthy spirits of boyhood were never treated brutally at Marlborough House. When Prince George and his elder brother were sent to the training-ship *Britannia* they showed " as much healthy naughtiness " as their contemporaries.

There is one enchanting story of a day when the Prince was taken with his brother to Westminster Abbey. Dean Stanley had been asked to show them the treasures of the Abbey. Nobody could make the memorials of Westminster come to life again as Dean Stanley could, with his vivid historic sense. In spite of the charm of the Dean's stories, Prince George wandered away by himself. At last he was found in a dim little side chapel. He had scrambled on top of Queen Elizabeth's tomb, and, looking down at the effigy, he was saying, " What an ugly old woman ! "

The Princess Alexandra proved herself more than motherly. There was nothing she enjoyed more than having the young princes romping in her presence. And Edward himself was a genial and interested father. Often he joined with their mother in ministering to the children's amusement. He is said to have left the House of Lords late one afternoon in the middle of an important speech, and to have written a hurried letter to the Lord Chancellor asking to be excused as he was celebrating his eldest girl's sixth birthday by taking the children to a circus.

One discovers that there was a healthy naughtiness in those two princes. George himself, because of his addiction to pranks and practical jokes, became known in the home circle as the " Royal Pickle."

Once at a family luncheon at Windsor Castle, in his childhood, he incurred the displeasure of the severe, as well as august Queen Victoria, and as a punishment was sent under the table until he was in a fit mind to behave himself.

After a while he was heard to say, " Grandmama, I'm quite good now."

" Very well, then," said Grandmama, " you may come out."

Out he came, wholly naked and unashamed, having in his banishment divested himself of every bit of clothing.

On this occasion Queen Victoria was distinctly amused.

Most of his boyhood was spent at Sandringham, that country house where he was, some seventy years later, peacefully to end his life.

Many royal children never know what a home means. In that respect Prince George was very fortunate. At Sandringham the daily round was scarcely different from that of any other English country house.

In London there was as little interference with home life as possible.

The boys were often their father's companions. They were constantly with their beautiful mother, and they both had for her a deep affection. At Sandringham, and on Deeside, they entered fully into all the activities of country and Highland life. Each year, too, they accompanied their parents to Copenhagen, and some of Prince George's best holidays were spent with his grandparents, the late King and Queen of Denmark.

Their father—marking the steady growth of the Empire, and, perhaps, with not too happy memories of his own boyhood's life—resolved that his sons should have a wholly different training. It was a period before kings and foreign royalties decided upon Eton as the real formative training of their sons. So Prince Edward informed Queen Victoria—who still took the keenest interest in the upbringing of the boys—that he intended to enter them as naval cadets on the *Britannia* at Portsmouth.

Her Majesty raised objections— many and various. She talked of the rough-and-tumble of a training-ship, the inability to pick and choose the comrades who would " chum " with her grandsons, the possibility of their forming acquaintances which it might be undesirable to retain in the future —all these and other considerations the Queen put forward in her forcible way. As a compromise, she even suggested Wellington College.

But the Prince of Wales was equally determined, and at length an agreement was arrived at. The boys' tutor, Mr. Dalton, would accompany them. The elder, of course, would not enter the Navy : Prince George would be free to do so, if he wished. Prince Albert

PRINCE GEORGE *with his bride and his grandmother, Queen Victoria. The Queen was delighted at the wedding, and frequently remarked that she was glad her grandson had such a good wife.*

Victor, Duke of Clarence, was a shy, rather melancholy boy, with not the best of health. Prince George was high-spirited, full of fun and often up to mischief.

So in 1877 they passed an examination—identical with that which every other candidate had to undergo—for naval cadetship, and served two years on the *Britannia*.

Prince George was twelve when he became the youngest cadet on board the *Britannia*. He was conscientious; the flame of duty, which was to be an inspiration of his reign, was already alive in him, and was an inheritance from his Coburg grandfather.

When he was a boy, there were already signs of the similarity in character. The signs were to increase as the years passed. But in leisure he was spirited and impish. On one occasion, a couple of marlinespikes found their way into the bed of an officer. A certain cadet was suspected. Then Prince George admitted that he was the culprit, and he faced his punishment. His leave was stopped for one week.

Nevertheless, the record of Prince George was that of an efficient officer. He was devotedly attached to his calling, although, like Nelson and other distinguished sailors, he suffered from seasickness. No distinction was made between Prince George and his shipmates. It has been recorded that he was an excellent singer of comic songs and often regaled his shipmates with the latest.

Moreover, he early displayed that keen sense of humour which remained with him always. Once when his ship was in Turkish waters, a Pasha came on board to pay his respects to the grandson of the Queen of England and son of the Prince of Wales. It happened that the Prince that day was having his turn in the duty of coaling, and when he appeared on deck, from the stokehold, his overalls black and his face and hands grimy with coal-dust, even the Oriental calm of the Pasha was ruffled at the sight.

It has been recalled that Prince George, as the youngest cadet ever placed on the books of the *Britannia*, was a very taking little sailor in his navy-blue uniform with gold buttons and cap-band. Perhaps because of his small size the other cadets named him " Sprat " ; while his taller and thinner brother was known as " Herring."

The life of the cadets was a very busy but a very happy one. Rising at half-past six, they bathed and dressed, and then had half an hour's drill, after which came breakfast. Studies of various kinds took up the morning from a quarter to nine till twelve o'clock.

After dinner they went ashore for an hour, returning to study at two, and keeping at it till four o'clock. The next two hours were usually devoted to sports or games of some kind ashore, and tea was served aboard at seven. Bedtime came at half-past nine, after another hour's study.

The food was good and nourishing, but plain and simply served. The boys throve upon it, growing and filling out satisfactorily, and becoming sturdy and manly in proportion to their age.

George seemed from the first cut out for a sailor. He quickly developed into a creditable oar, pulling more than once in a winning crew in the cadets' rowing-matches. In the more intricate though less arduous pastime of boat

AN UNUSUAL PHOTOGRAPH *of Prince George fishing in Scotland. From boyhood he was fond of outdoor pursuits.*

PRINCE GEORGE *with a favourite dog.   He was always a great dog lover, and many of his dogs have won prizes at important shows.*

sailing he was conspicuously successful, winning prizes in open competition.

The presentation of prizes was usually made a gala occasion, some important personage being asked to present the rewards to the victors. Edward and Alexandra consented to perform this ceremony while their sons were under the charge of Captain Fairfax, and were rowed to the *Britannia* in the royal galley, Prince George pulling the second bow oar and Prince Victor holding the tiller.

There is no doubt that the thorough training which the future King George received on board the *Britannia* had a tremendous effect upon his character in the future. From those days he learned the necessity for punctuality, regular habits, and an orderliness that never left him for the rest of his life.

Furthermore, it bred in him that love for the sea and his acute knowledge of naval matters that caused unusual trepidation in Admiralty quarters when it was learned that King George desired to inspect his fleet. The Sea Lords knew that a real sailor was inspecting sailors.

When this period was approaching its end, the Prince of Wales, having obtained the Queen's assent, disclosed to the First Lord of the Admiralty his desire that the two princes should see the world in a literal sense—on board a ship of the Royal Navy.

Mr. W. H. Smith, nicknamed " Old Morality," was not a little disturbed at so startling an innovation. He communicated his fears to the Cabinet, which seems to have shared his views ; for the Prime Minister wrote to the Queen. He pointed out that the project, if carried out, would " greatly disquiet the public mind," and " if anything happened to them " the Government would be " justly called to account."

This was one of Lord Beaconsfield's very few mistakes in his dealing with the Monarch. The matter was one, he was told, with which the Cabinet had no concern, and he received a Royal rebuke. " I entirely approve the plan," the Queen telegraphed, " which ought never to have been brought before the Cabinet. The Prince of Wales only mentioned it to Mr. Smith, and was, with right, extremely annoyed at his doing so. Such a thing was never done when the Prince of Wales and Prince Alfred went on long journeys and voyages."

So Prince George began a series of Empire and world tours which made him the most travelled of all monarchs, and laid the foundations of that wise understanding which was to prove of such value in later life.

The princes served on the *Bacchante* for three years ; were treated in the same way as their messmates ; took their turns of duty in all weathers ; and only when ashore did they receive those marks of attention due to their Royal rank.

Mr. (later Canon) Dalton—promoted from tutor to governor—went with them, superintended their studies (an addition to their work on board), and edited their diary, which was subsequently published.

IV

So the two young princes were, on September 17, 1879, transferred to the *Bacchante* to begin their world tour. The *Bacchante* herself was an epitome of old and new. In her armament were included a muzzle-loading broadside and Whitehead torpedo tubes. She could, furthermore, bowl along at a stately six knots—or frequently more—under sail, or dip screw into water in a more up-to-date fashion.

There was no hint yet that Prince George would become heir to the Throne, through his elder brother's death. He was therefore educated as a second son, with the consequent differences in aims and responsibilities. A sailor's life suited him ; he was a man's man, and his character and tastes were of the mould that thrives in a wardroom or an officers' mess.

In the *Bacchante* the princes travelled as far as Australia and New Zealand. In Australia they descended a gold mine ; they aimed with boomerangs, and even ate minced kangaroo. In New Zealand they shook hands with dusky Maori chieftains who had fought against their grandmother's soldiers.

Prince George was at home on both land and sea. He wrote in his Journal : " After dinner much amusement, trying to sit on an empty corked bottle, on the deck, at the same time holding a candle in each hand, one of which was lighted, the other to be lighted from it, without rolling over."

While he was in Australian waters Prince George left the *Bacchante* to stay with an Australian hostess. She made a charming gesture which showed him that graciousness was to flourish as well as corn and wool in the new countries of his grandmother's empire. When he went down for breakfast he found a wreath of rosebuds about his plate. They were, he was told, " For Sunday morning and in memory of England."

It was during this voyage that the world was startled by a statement widely published in the newspapers that the princes, landing at Bermuda, had each had his nose tattooed with an anchor. It was feared in the Royal Household that the story might be true, because of Prince George's addiction to pranks and practical jokes. There was no knowing what a boy like that might be up to. Anxious messages were sent to the ship and, greatly to the relief of the country as well as of the Royal Family, it was announced that the story was unfounded.

What had happened was that the boys ornamented each other's noses with pollen from the brilliant orange stamens of the Bermuda lilies. From that day to this yellow noses are regarded as the height of fashion in the island, especially by the native ladies.

It was also while a midshipman that Prince George began his hobby of stamp collecting, which remained one of his chief relaxations. It can be said that the late King George possessed one of the most comprehensive and valuable collections of stamps in the world. It was an excellent hobby for a boy to have chosen. Postage stamps do give a breadth of vision, with the vivid colouring, the heads of potentates, the pictures and names of far-off places suggestive of romance. As the King once told the Junior Philatelic Society, it was a hobby he had pursued with " unabated interest " throughout the years.

Before he left home for this world voyage he promised his mother to read the Bible daily. The Pocket Testament League in 1912 wrote to Buckingham Palace asking if it was true that King George followed the practice of daily Bible reading.

THERE WAS GREAT NATIONAL REJOICING *when their first son, Prince Edward, was born on June 23, 1894. This event gave the Throne three generations in direct line of accession.*

A GROUP *taken on the Royal yacht at the Naval Review during the celebration of Queen Victoria's Diamond Jubilee,* 1897. *The late King Edward, surrounded by his eldest son, the Duke of Edinburgh, Prince Henry of Prussia, King of Denmark, and Prince Louis of Battenberg.*

" It is quite true," Lord Knollys, the King's Private Secretary, replied, " that he promised Queen Alexandra as long ago as 1881 that he would read a chapter of the Bible daily, and that he has ever since adhered to this promise."

Always the watchful eye of Queen Victoria was on the young princes. When the *Bacchante*, in which her grandsons were serving as midshipmen, had been ordered to South Africa, where trouble was brewing, Queen Victoria wrote to her daughter-in-law, Alexandra :

" DARLING ALIX,

" I am sorry Bertie [the future King Edward] should have been sore about the boys ; but I think he must have forgotten the arrangements and conditions and instructions respecting their going to sea.

" I, and even Bertie and you, only consented to their both going to sea for their education and moral training. This being the case—the *Bacchante* going to the Cape, which was done in a hurry without one consultation with me (I disapproved)—and feeling how valuable these two young lives are to the whole nation, I felt bound to protect them against useless and unnecessary exposure in a cruel Civil war—for so it is, the Boers being my subjects, and it being a rule that Princes of the Royal Family ought not to be mixed in it.

" In any other war, should in time there be one (when Georgie be older), and his ship be obliged to take part in it, I would quite agree with Bertie.

" Pray show this to him, as I am sure he and everyone would agree in this being the right course."

But even Queen Victoria could not control the adventures which the young princes encountered on this world tour.

The ship nearly drowned Prince George in the Pacific upon one occasion. They even survived the adventure with a mad native of Simonstown, who almost killed them in a " spider " drawn by four beautiful white horses, which the Governor had sent over to drive them to Cape Town.

Mad with drink, we are told, the native drove headlong up hill and down dale, into the surf of the sea and out of it, crashed into a Cape wagon, and finished upon the spoke of one wheel at Government House, a jubilant man who was at least an optimist.

And in this same region, when sailing round the Cape of Good Hope, our future King and some of those who sailed with him in the *Bacchante* fell in with a phantom ship and clearly observed that her spars and her sails shone with a fire as of gold.

At the end of the cruise, in 1882, the two brothers parted company. Prince Albert Victor was destined for the Army and the succession to the Throne ; Prince George adopted the sea as his avocation. His Englishry was already marked. Truly he could say :

I travelled among unknown men,
In lands beyond the sea ;
Nor, England, did I know till then
What love I bore to thee.

Prince George was given his first independent command—Torpedo Boat No. 79. This ship took part in the naval manœuvres of 1889 in some of the worst weather which has ever been experienced on our coasts.

Admiral Penrose Fitzgerald has brought to light an incident in these manœuvres which shows that the King was not only a capable but a very plucky sailor. Three torpedo boats, of which No. 79 was one, had a rendezvous with a senior officer in Lough Swilly.

Prince George's little craft turned up in time, but had to report the grave news that one of its companions had engine trouble and had been obliged to anchor close to the Donegal coast. The commander of No. 79 reported that he had tried to tow the crippled torpedo boat, but his towing gear had broken. There was nothing to be done except to leave her with the third torpedo boat standing by and report at the rendezvous for fresh hawsers.

The senior naval officer wanted to go to the rescue himself, but with some misgivings gave way to the request of the plucky young commander of No. 79 to let him have another try. A less conscientious commander might well have rested satisfied after spending the previous night in trying to assist his companion ship, and leave to a crew less tired than his own, the task of dealing with the situation. The future King was, however, made of sterner stuff, so, equipped with a new hawser, he put to sea again in the teeth of a heavy gale.

The work of rescuing the disabled torpedo boat was a job requiring not only courage and initiative, but skilful seamanship, and one of those proud moments which the King must have loved to recall was when he towed the helpless ship to safety. The incident reveals that the King was in his true element when at sea, and there is reality behind the proud title " Sailor King."

For this achievement Prince George received the post of commander of the first-class gunboat *Thrush*, and later commander of the new second-class cruiser *Melampus*. This commission was designed to be the first of a series of important commands. There was no doubt of the keenness of Prince George. His ambition was that one day he would have the pride and joy of hoisting his Flag as an Admiral on the active list. He used to say how glad he was that he would not have to be King, as he wanted to remain a sailor.

Fate, however, decreed that this command of the *Melampus* was to be his last naval appointment as Prince George. In November 1891 he was attacked by serious illness, which very nearly brought to an end his career.

The Prince was on a visit to the Curragh, where his brother was quartered with his regiment, the 11th Hussars. He returned to a small family party at Sandringham, but showed signs of being seriously ill. He developed fever, and his father hurried him off to London, where the doctors diagnosed enteric fever.

It was a long struggle, but Prince George came through. His vigorous and healthy constitution resisted the disease germs. But the young Prince had only entered upon the convalescent stage when another tragic event occurred in the English Royal Family, which was to change entirely the outlook of Prince George.

In January 1892, by the premature death of his brother Prince Albert Victor, Duke of Clarence, he came into the direct line of succession to the Throne. After sixteen years' continuous service afloat, his career at sea was abruptly terminated. He was raised to the peerage as Duke of York,

A PHOTOGRAPH *taken soon after their marriage.*

FOUR SOVEREIGNS. *Queen Victoria, Edward VII, George V, and Edward VIII.*

IN ELIZABETHAN COSTUME *at a ball at Devonshire House*, 1897.

and was introduced in the House of Lords by his father.

A new and greater career was opening for him.

V

And so we come to the woman, the first lady of the land, who has played an important and great part in this drama of the life of King George the Fifth.

Queen Mary is undoubtedly the most gracious, the most dignified, and most important Queen Mother in the world to-day. She has endeared herself to the people of this country in no uncertain fashion. She is admired and esteemed, and there is no member of any royal household who takes the duties of royalty so seriously, or who works harder at what is perhaps the most exacting job in the world.

Queen Mary may be said to be a real Londoner. She was born on the stroke of midnight, May 26, 1867, in Kensington Palace, in a room which had been the nursery of Queen Victoria. She is descended from Adolphus, Duke of Cambridge, the seventh son of George III, who married the Princess Augusta, the daughter of the Landgrave of Hesse. The Queen's mother, the Princess Marie Adelaide, was the second daughter of the Duke of Cambridge, and therefore the cousin and a contemporary of Queen Victoria, but some fourteen years her junior.

At her baptism, by the Archbishop of Canterbury, she was given a garland of names—Victoria Mary Augusta Louisa Olga Pauline Claudine Agnes —only to have them all reduced to May, the name by which she was affectionately known long before she came to the Throne.

" A pretty child she was, with fair hair and blue eyes—very English looking," the Palace gatekeeper's wife said of her, remembering the child who was so inquisitive about the names of the flowers in the garden.

Princess May, as the future Queen Mary was known, had three brothers. At the time the Teck family were by no means wealthy. Because of a financial crisis they had to economise drastically. After a time Kensington Palace had to be given up, and then a period of exile in Italy was found necessary. For some eighteen months the Princess May studied in Florence under an Italian governess, and had lessons from a painting master.

It was a time when women were emerging from their almost harem-like seclusion and acting and thinking for themselves. A quiet, sure revolution with none of the hysterics and sensationalism which later were to be embodied in the Suffragette movement in Britain.

Princess May was eager to develop her mental and intellectual qualities. She displayed an eager desire for knowledge. Helped by her Alsatian governess, Madame Bricka, she began a self-imposed task of six hours' serious reading each day. The decision was made in 1886, the year when she was seen on her appearance as a débutante.

Bricka, the Alsatian governess, was a dominating character. She taught her young charge the importance of differentiating between the trivial and the important. The Empire owes much to that passionate, resolute, dark Alsatian woman, for Madame Bricka may be said to have moulded the character of our Queen Mother.

Queen Mary has known what it is

AN HISTORIC PHOTOGRAPH taken at Osborne, where Queen Victoria was giving a family party. Queen Mary (third from left) is holding Prince Albert, and Prince Edward is by her side.

PRINCE GEORGE *with his father, the late King Edward, whilst out shooting.*

PHOTOGRAPHED IN 1902, just after his return from a Dominion tour, with Princes
Edward, Albert, and Henry, and Princess Mary.

to be poor—really poor. When her father and mother lived at White Lodge, Richmond, they could not afford a carriage. Because it was the Victorian age and they were royalty, they had to have one. And so economies of the most stringent nature were absolutely necessary inside the house.

But Queen Victoria, with her passion for arranging the affairs of the Royal House, had already decided that Princess May should enter the Royal circle. Under the watchful eye of the great Queen the young princess was encouraged to be studious, serious, and sedate. She was taught to read well and speak well.

Rumour said that she was shy and retiring, a contrast to the kindly, beloved bustling Duchess of Teck, whom she often accompanied on philanthropic errands to the poor. She learnt the businesslike running of a household, getting a first-hand knowledge of that domestic art known as " making both ends meet."

Besides her course of serious reading, the future Queen studied music under Tosti, who found her an apt and amenable pupil. Her voice was a sweet but light soprano, which was unfortunately never heard outside the family circle.

But despite her life on the Continent and the opportunities she had of meeting many famous people, Princess May lived a life much different from that of the modern young woman on the Continent, drifting from Le Touquet to the Lido in a luxury cocktail tour. Her life was one of almost strict retirement.

This failure to extend her early circle of acquaintances may be due to the fact that all her life the Queen has not made friends easily. One of her best-informed biographers says : " In a less exalted circle, with fewer opportunities of coming into contact with every possible variety of temperament, she would probably have been a very lonely woman, but once she makes a friend, the friendship is a steadfast and enduring affection ; she does not invite confidences, but in time of trouble she is a staunch and loyal supporter of those who have claims upon her."

Both Queen Victoria and the Princess of Wales (afterwards Queen Alexandra) developed a great affection and profound admiration for the reserved and beautiful daughter of the gay and debonair Duchess of Teck. She seemed marked out for greatness, and her engagement to the Duke of Clarence, the second in succession to the Throne, was received with no surprise, and, indeed, with immense public enthusiasm.

This betrothal was announced in November 1891. Then came the tragedy. The Duke died five weeks before the date of the wedding. Prince George, still convalescent from his own illness, became the heir presumptive to the Throne.

The untimely death of the handsome young prince was looked upon as a national calamity. To Princess May it was a terrible blow. After the funeral she fled with her parents to White Lodge, Richmond, where she could think in quietness of the future and what it might have in store. Later, she went to France with her mother to get over the blow. At the same time, she did not forget the Princess of Wales, who was genuinely overcome with grief and sorrow at the death

5

of her eldest son, for whom she had the deepest affection.

But, many months later, it was rumoured that Prince George was now paying court to the popular princess. There came the occasion when a family council was held at Windsor Castle to discuss the proposed marriage of Princess May and Prince George. Queen Victoria presided, and some shrewd comments were made by the subsequent King Edward VII.

Perhaps the preliminary tragedy of the death of the Duke of Clarence overshadowed and to some extent prevented the romantic courtship which the public delights upon in royal engagements. Nevertheless, when the future King asked her hand in marriage, Princess May replied : " I shall do my best to make you happy."

It cannot be said that she has failed. She has made herself the most dignified Queen in Europe, respected throughout the world. And her unswerving loyalty to England and its future has endeared her to all in the land.

There was genuine delight throughout the country when it was announced that the " Sailor Prince " had " made his own choice " and was to marry Princess May, a daughter of England. The engagement brought the congratulations of the Empire.

The Times expressed the popular feeling by saying : " We have the satisfaction of making the announcement for which the public will not be wholly unprepared. The understanding so long reported to exist between the Duke of York and Princess May has now taken the form of a definite betrothal, which has received the ready sanction of Her Majesty the Queen. We are certain that this intelligence

will be received with sincere gratification.

" In the peculiar circumstances attending such a union there must perforce be present in every mind a certain conflict of emotions. But the predominant feeling, now that a sufficient interval has elapsed since the melancholy death of the Duke of Clarence, will be that this betrothal accords with the fitness of things, and, so far from offending any legitimate sentiment, is the most appropriate and delicate medicament for the wound, in its nature never wholly ineffaceable. There is even ground for hoping that a union rooted in painful memories may prove happy beyond the common lot. The persons of both parties are such as to attract sympathy. On the one hand, the Duke of York enjoys not only the popularity attaching to the Navy, but also a personal good will, founded on his own frank and manly bearing on the occasions when he has come before the public. The Princess May is endeared to the public by her personal charm and her amiable disposition, by the memory of her bereavement, and still more by the devotion she displayed at that trying juncture. . . ."

King Edward took control of the wedding arrangements, though they had, of course, to be approved by Queen Victoria. King Edward was a first-rate hand at arranging big ceremonials and enjoyed it.

The wedding ceremony was a splendid affair at the Chapel Royal, St. James's. Queen Victoria attended in full state, and every nation in the world sent either its monarch or heir to the throne to do honour to the future King and Queen of England.

Queen Victoria, apparently as enthusiastic as the other members of her family, started out for the church considerably before the time appointed for the ceremony, actually arriving there before the officers of State. Driving along in her carriage, drawn by the famous cream ponies, the aged monarch was received by the excited crowd with every sign of affection and regard, and descending at the church door, she walked quietly into the chapel, which was decorated entirely in white, and ascended the dais at the side of the altar.

There were ten bridesmaids, the Duke of Edinburgh being the best man. The whole scene was one which for splendour and magnificence has rarely been equalled. The Duke of Teck gave away his daughter. From the organ came the wedding march from *Lohengrin*. The Archbishop of Canterbury performed the ceremony, and Princess May had become the Duchess of York.

London was *en fête* throughout the whole day. The illuminations at night were on a scale of magnificence never before equalled. Some of the rejoicing crowd made their way in the afternoon to the front of St. James's Palace, and cheered till Prince George appeared at the window. He came forth on to a balcony. The crowd cheered louder than ever. It was impossible for him to make his voice heard above the roar, so he seized a light chair standing near and waved it above his head to show his sympathy with the rejoicing of the crowd. Some of the wilder spirits instantly shouted out : " Throw it down to us ! " Laughing heartily, the Prince seemed about to comply with their request when his newly-married Princess put her hand on his arm and smilingly shook her head.

Later, the Duke and Duchess of York drove in procession from the Palace to Liverpool Street Railway Station, and took train for Sandringham for the honeymoon at York Cottage. In the streets through which they passed were gathered huge crowds of cheering people. The 3,500 wedding presents came from all parts of the Empire.

And, at the end of it all, a lone figure was seen leaning over a balcony railing in St. James's Palace, smoking a cigarette and looking rather forlorn. It was the Duke of Teck, father of the future Queen of England.

CHAPTER III

FIRST YEARS OF MARRIAGE

Birth of Prince Edward and Prince Albert—Royal duties—Queen Victoria's death—Raised to Duke of Cornwall—A tour of the Empire—Widespread enthusiasm and loyalty.

I

ONCE married, the Royal couple settled down to a life of quiet domesticity, which was, for the most part, their general desire.

York House, in St. James's Palace, was a convenient and handsome residence in town, and York Cottage, if hardly a " stately domain," was sufficiently near to Sandringham House to be a welcome residence in Norfolk. It had served hitherto as an " overflow " annexe for those bachelor guests King Edward liked to have about him ; but now it was to become rather a nursery than a guest-house . . . so that, as Sir George Arthur has told us, King George ultimately was moved to exclaim : " I shall soon have a regiment, not a family."

The future King Edward VIII was born at White Lodge. The patron saints of England, Scotland, Ireland, and Wales were evoked at the baptism of the infant, who was destined to be the twentieth Prince of Wales, and for the first time in history a Queen Regnant held in her arms her descendant in the fourth generation.

It was little wonder that the birth of Edward Albert Christian George Andrew Patrick David was hailed with joy. Not since Tudor times, when Jane Seymour presented Henry VIII

with the sickly infant who was to become Edward VI, had an heir to the Throne been born in England of parents who gloried in their English birth.

Apropos of this baptism, we have recently had the story given by Lord Esher, Constable of Windsor. Lord Esher once sat next the future King George at dinner on the Royal yacht.

" He [George] mentioned a queer prophecy which he made me promise I would not repeat to the King [Edward] who is rather influenced by these old women's tales. Someone, about forty years ago, said of the late Queen that she would have a long and glorious reign, the longest and most glorious of all the English sovereigns ; that she would be succeeded by two kings who would have short reigns, and by a third whose name would be David and whose name would be as glorious as hers. One of Prince Edward's names is David !

" When Lady Waterford was dying she sent for the Prince of Wales and implored him to call his then unborn son David, as she had some fad about restoring the Jews to the Holy City. To humour her, he consented, and Prince Edward was given the names of the four patron saints of England, Scotland, Ireland, and Wales—i.e. George, Andrew, Patrick, David."

And that prophecy was twenty years

PRINCE GEORGE *in the uniform of the Isle of Wight Rifles.*

WITH THE SHAH OF PERSIA *during his State visit to England in* 1902.

or more before the British themselves went to Palestine !

The date of this auspicious birth was June 23, 1894. The Princess of Wales and the Duchess of Teck were at White Lodge, Richmond, for the happy event. Queen Victoria came two days later to see the infant who had thus become Her Majesty's third direct heir. Hundreds of messages of congratulations reached Prince George and his wife.

On December 14, 1895, the Duke and Duchess rejoiced in the birth of their second son. To the Lord Mayor of London the Duke telegraphed from York Cottage : " I am deeply touched by the kind congratulations and good wishes you send from the citizens of London. I thank them with all my heart.—GEORGE." The infant Prince made excellent progress, and was baptised in the names of Albert Frederick Arthur George. The little Prince's birth served to brighten the sad memories of December 14, which was the anniversary of the death of both the Prince Consort and Queen Victoria's beloved daughter, Princess Alice.

The Duke and Duchess paid several visits during the year to different parts of the country. They opened a new infirmary at Lancaster, this being the first Royal visit since Queen Victoria received " the keys of the ancient castle " fifty years ago. In responding to a toast, the Prince, mindful of the old Wars of the Roses, said wittily that four hundred years ago a Duke of York would never have thought of bringing his wife to Lancaster !

They journeyed next day to Salford, and opened a fine technical institute erected at a cost of £70,000. After staying with the Earl and Countess of Derby they drove through Liverpool and took a trip on the overhead electric railway, cheered by many thousands in the streets.

On April 25, 1897, to the great joy of the Duke and Duchess, a daughter was born to them. She received the names of Victoria Alexandra Alice Mary, and from the earliest days of her life grew a sturdy and healthy child. Being the only girl in the family, she has naturally been a special favourite with her parents and brothers.

In June came the marvellous Diamond Jubilee with all its worldwide tributes of love and honour to Queen Victoria. The Duke and Duchess of York participated in the celebrations and accompanied the venerated Sovereign to the thanksgiving service outside St. Paul's Cathedral. The announcement that the Duke and Duchess would pay a visit to Ireland drew forth a gratifying response in that country. They spent ten days at Cowes in July before starting for the long series of engagements across the Irish Channel. A previous Royal visit was recalled by one of the speakers, who said, at a representative meeting to prepare for the Royal visit, that he was old enough to remember the visit of George IV in 1821 !

The Duke and Duchess started from London on August 17, and crossed in bad weather. An extraordinary welcome greeted them—even greater, it was said, than that accorded in London to Queen Victoria on her Jubilee. The sun shone brilliantly, as if to atone for the roughness of the voyage, and the vessels in Kingstown Harbour were dressed rainbow fashion. The splendid procession through the streets was received with " a genuine Irish welcome." The Viceroy, Lord Cadogan, and Field-

PRINCE GEORGE *out shooting. It was always his favourite hobby, and he was rated as one of the ten best shots in England.*

ANOTHER PHOTOGRAPH *of him out shooting pheasants, taken at Brocket Hall, Hatfield.*

A PHOTOGRAPH taken at Cowes during the visit of the Tsar and Tsarina in 1909. King
Edward VII is in the centre, and the Tsar and Tsarina are on each side of him. King
George is at the right, nursing one of the Tsar's daughters.

Marshal Lord Roberts were among the most noticeable personages next to the Royal Party. The Duchess wore a dress of green Irish poplin with a toque of green poplin and pink roses. Her smiling face evoked wonderful enthusiasm. The next day was a repetition — " There is a pitch of national enthusiasm which cannot be surpassed," said *The Times*. A State visit was paid to the Irish Textile Exhibition, and the Duchess looked thoroughly at the embroidery and needlework, lingering quite a long time to admire the various specimens of Irish lace and drawn-thread work.

The Irish love horses, and the Royal guests were loudly applauded on their way to the races at Leopardstown Park. On Sunday they worshipped in the little parish church at Howth. During the following week they were present at the great Horse Show ; stayed with Lord and Lady Iveagh ; saw the charms of Bray, and did much sightseeing in Dublin. The Duke reviewed the assembly of the Boys' Brigade in Phœnix Park. A splendid garden-party at the Viceregal Lodge gave Dublin society yet another opportunity of witnessing the graciousness of the Duke and the Duchess.

On August 28 their Royal Highnesses commenced a visit to Killarney, but the lake was too rough to allow them to venture on it. Next day the Duke had some shooting in Lord Kenmare's deer forest, bringing down a wild red deer, and the Duchess was able to embark in a State barge on the lake. They saw Valencia Harbour and stayed a short while with Lord Dunraven. On one or two days the rain was almost incessant, but the courage of the Duchess was equal to the occasion, and she would not disappoint the crowds that were " watching out " for her. " The Irish air agrees with me amazingly," she said. From Newton Stewart they went to Londonderry, a town with a romantic story indeed. When Their Royal Highnesses concluded their visit to Ireland, it was with the knowledge that they had stirred the liveliest feelings of loyalty and had won for themselves an affection which would be lasting.

The Prince sent a letter to the Viceroy, saying : " The agreeable impressions which we have derived from our visit can never be effaced from our memory." Queen Victoria telegraphed, saying how pleased she had been to hear of the " very loyal and kind reception my dear grandchildren have met with everywhere in Ireland."

The only cloud on the happiness of this memorable visit was the unsatisfactory news of the health of the Duchess of Teck, who had become perceptibly weaker since April. Between mother and daughter there had always been maintained a regular correspondence, and the Duchess of York heard with anxiety of her mother's increased weakness. At the end of April the Duchess of Teck became decidedly worse, and an operation was considered necessary. It was successful, and the Duchess received an especially warm welcome from the crowds on Jubilee Day. The popular Duchess performed a few more public duties, and her cheerfulness encouraged her family to hope that she might be spared for many years. But on October 25 she was taken ill, and Mr. Allingham performed another operation. The brave-hearted Duchess did her utmost to cheer her distressed husband and children when she rallied again to consciousness, but the end came swiftly on October 27, when she passed away in the presence of the Duke of Teck, the Duchess of York, and Prince Alexander of Teck. Prince Adolphus, who had been staying at Eaton Hall, arrived soon after the sad event.

The shadows of the South African War were settling on the Empire, and Queen Victoria did all in her power to hearten her people by her presence in their midst. All the Royal Family were affected by the news from South Africa, for many of the officers who lost their lives had been personal friends of theirs.

In January 1900, the Duke of Teck passed away, at the age of sixty-two. His last years had been overclouded by weakness and an entire loss of interest in life. To the Duchess of York his death was a great grief, although her father's condition had been one which allowed no hope of recovery.

On March 31, 1900, another son was born to the Duke and Duchess. He was named Henry William Frederick Albert.

The future Queen Mary soon revealed herself as a devoted mother. She did her utmost to implant in her children her own love of reading and serious interest in art and literature. The Duke of York, however, seems to be the only one of her children who developed the studious habits of his mother.

This younger generation of the House of Hanover, as it was then, interested Lord Esher. He wrote in his diary :

" I was amused to-day by taking the Wales children, two boys and a girl, to the Abbey. They climbed on to every tomb and got very dirty, but were thoroughly happy . . . Prince Edward remarked of the Duke of Buckingham that he was a ' wicked man,' and when I asked why, he said he gave bad advice to Charles I. He knew that Buckingham had been murdered at Portsmouth by Felton. I think he must have been reading Dumas ! "

" The girl," of course, was Princess Mary, now Countess of Harewood.

Lord Esher could not help comparing " the boys " with each other. " The second boy," he wrote, " is the sharpest "—a nice compliment to the Duke of York—" but there is something rather taking about Prince Edward. He wants a walking-stick with a horse's head on it for his birthday."

II

So the end of the great Queen Victoria was near. She was eighty, and tired of all the pomp and circumstance. It was the year 1901. The long-continued strain of the South African War weighed heavily on the heart of the Sovereign, whose grief for " my poor soldiers " had been expressed in a hundred touching forms. Many a sorrowing relative of a gallant soldier was comforted in those dark days by a personal message from the aged Queen.

She herself had been bereaved in 1900, for in that year her son, the Duke of Saxe-Coburg-Gotha, died in July at the age of fifty-six ; the Duke of Teck died in January ; and the gallant Prince Christian Victor laid down his life at Pretoria. The last-

A GROUP SHOWING KING GEORGE AND QUEEN MARY. *Standing on each side of the King are Sir John French and Sir Philip Chetwode. Lady French is on the Queen's right.*

PRINCE GEORGE *wisely decided upon educating his eldest son along the same lines as he had been educated. Consequently Prince Edward became a cadet at Osborne College in* 1907.

A CHARMING PICTURE *of Queen Mary with her youngest son, George.*

KING GEORGE *with his son and namesake, Prince George.*

A HAPPY PICTURE *of King Edward VII with his eldest son, Prince of Wales, at Epsom in* 1909, *when his horse won the Derby.*

6

A FAMILY LUNCHEON PARTY AT SANDRINGHAM. *King George can be seen with his mother, Queen Alexandra, and Queen Mary.*

named was an especial favourite with Her Majesty, and his pathetic request to his parents that if he fell he should be buried on the battlefield was characteristic of his soldierly spirit.

Queen Victoria's illness was mercifully brief, though even that week sufficed to prove, as Mr. Balfour remarked, how industrious the Sovereign's life had been and how great was the accumulation of only a few day's business of State.

She excused herself from meeting her Ministers. They would argue with her, and she would say, " You know I cannot any longer argue." Even her secretaries were kept at a distance. Ladies-in-waiting read the papers to her and brought down messages from her room which led to " complications."

She made a brave fight of it. At Netley Hospital there were two wounded soldiers to be decorated with the Victoria Cross. They were " sitting in chairs," and when the Queen was wheeled in " they were ordered to rise." But the Queen said, " Most certainly not." Without help—" a very unusual thing "—she raised herself " and stood over them while she decorated them."

So we come to the final drama, which must be described in Lord Esher's own words. This historic passage is as follows :

" The dying scene was stately and dramatic. The Queen now and then recognised those about her and spoke their names. Her difficulty in breathing was the only painful symptom. Reid—the doctor—passed his arm around her and supported her.

" The King knelt at the side of the bed. The German Emperor stood silently at the head, near the Queen. The other children and grandchildren were there, calling their names to her at intervals. She died quite peacefully. After the King had left for London the Emperor took charge of everything, so unlike what was expected of him.

" He refused to allow Banting's men (the undertakers) to measure the Queen for her shell. He turned them out of the room. He sent for Reid, and took all the measurements himself. He and the King and the Duke of Connaught lifted the Queen into her coffin.

" The day before her death, while the Prince of Wales was in the house, but not allowed to go near the Queen for fear of alarming her, she said : ' The Prince of Wales will be sorry to hear how ill I am. Do you think he ought to be told ? ' Another thing she said was : ' I don't want to die yet. There are several things I want to arrange.' "

So ended the great reign on January 22, 1901, and for a time all was confusion. People who ought to have known had forgotten the precedents to be followed.

At Windsor, Esher would see the Indian attendants of the dead Queen no longer " statuesque," but " wandering about like uneasy spirits "—and, if we may add a few details to the picture, what a house-cleaning there had to be ! An Oriental trophy in the Waterloo Gallery was touched—out flew a cloud of moths, and the trophy had to be burned in the courtyard. Tons of ivory, delivered as tribute by an African chief, were rotting in an attic. Huge supplies of plates with royal portraits on them, which had been intended to give away as presents, were quietly disposed of. An immense paraphernalia of illuminated addresses, silver trowels, and other gifts had to be quietly obliterated.

Lord Esher felt the change from the " mystery and awe of the old court."

" Somehow," he wrote, " the sanctity of the Throne has disappeared." Dinner was served in the Edwardian style —not in the oak dining-room, but in a room all white—and " the quiet impressive entrance of the Queen into the corridor is as obsolete as Queen Elizabeth." Guests assembled in the green drawing-room and King Edward just walked in.

With King Edward's accession to the Throne a great change came to the household of Prince George and Mary. The real training of Prince George for the Kingship, which was to follow, now began. He became Duke of Cornwall, but was not given the title of Prince of Wales for some months.

It was at that time he began to study matters more closely related to the high office to which he was ultimately to be called—the working of the English Constitution and the various departments of public life— and he did it, as was his manner, with quiet, unostentatious, and thorough diligence.

During the ten years of the reign of King Edward, he was, as Prince of Wales, the companion and coadjutor of his father in the business of government. This was an experience which few Kings of England have had, although later the Prince of Wales did not hesitate to shoulder such burdens of State as came his way, and during the first illness of King George, relieved him of many tiring ceremonial duties.

It may be interesting to insert here a portion of the speech made by the new King at this time to his first Council in St. James's Palace, since, in a later chapter, the first speech of King George after his accession will also be quoted.

" In undertaking the heavy load which now devolves upon me," said King Edward VII, " I am fully determined to be a Constitutional Sovereign in the strictest sense of the word, and, as long as there is a breath in my body, to work for the good and amelioration of my people."

The King's anxieties were at this time very greatly increased by the illness of Prince George, who was attacked by German measles, and was unable to attend Queen Victoria's funeral. Happily the disease took a favourable turn, and the Prince, speedily recovering, was able to start on March 16 in the *Ophir*, on a great historical tour of the British Dominions.

III

The cruise of the *Ophir* marked a new stage in the development of Empire relations. That brilliant writer of the day, Mr. Rudyard Kipling, may have revealed the Empire to itself and a few bewildered people in Britain. But it was left to Prince George to teach the Empire something about Britain and, incidentally, impress the Kiplingesque message on the minds of the people of England when he returned.

It was a time when Britain was only just discovering its own wide-flung and rather haphazardly acquired Empire.

A good deal of that territory had come under the rule of the British Crown with many misgivings and obvious reluctance on the part of the statesmen responsible for what has been described as " British colonisation of the world." It is a fact often forgotten in these days when European nations seeking world expansion accuse Britain of a greedy and bloody policy of acquisitions during the reigns of Victoria and Edward VII.

Actually, Britain stepped into territories to restore peace and order where the archangels of European Chancelleries feared to tread. And it remained for sovereigns to prove by gestures, speeches, tours, and constitutional grants of self-government, that Britain has, for the most part, been disinterested and yet always helpful in those territories into which Victorian and Edwardian statesmanship led them so reluctantly.

Embarking on the *Ophir* at Portsmouth on March 16, Prince George and Princess Mary sailed first to Gibraltar, H.M.S. *Diadem* and *Niobe* escorting them to the entry of the Straits and there delivering over their charge to the *Andromeda* and *Diana*. The town of Gibraltar was *en fête* ; triumphal arches had been erected, and everything possible done to show honour to the representatives of His Majesty.

From Gibraltar the *Ophir* steamed eastward to Malta, and thence to Port Said. An impressive sight she must have been, especially at night-time, when, with her two attendant warships, she glided like a mighty glow-worm across the dark waters of the Mediterranean.

Her deck houses were of two stories, and lighted throughout by electricity, and the portholes below them, large and square, gave out also in fine weather a flood of radiance. In the daytime her white paintwork and gleaming brass glittering and winking in the sunshine made her a picture delightful to gaze upon, especially in contrast with the grim, black-hulled warships which followed, one upon the port quarter and the other on the starboard, at a distance of half a mile or so.

The welcome given to the Royal tourists at Malta was distinguished not only by its enthusiasm but its many unique features. Sir John Fisher and the officers of his fleet had invented, and their artificers had contrived, a remarkable marine menagerie of sea-monsters, including a mighty sea-serpent and a dolphin at least forty feet in length. The natives of the island came in their hundreds to welcome the Duke and Duchess at Verdala Palace ; and the civil and military dignitaries did their utmost to make the occasion memorable in the annals of the historic island.

The voyage through the Suez Canal and down the Red Sea was uneventful, and Aden was reached at seven o'clock on the morning of April 7, which happened to be Good Friday. Here the *Juno* and *St. George*, which were to accompany her to Australia, were awaiting the Royal yacht, and they and the guardship *Racoon* were manned and dressed to welcome her, thundering out in company with the shore batteries a salute of thirty-one guns.

The town of Aden itself cannot be seen from the harbour, spreading as it does over a broad plateau shut in by steep and rugged cliffs of volcanic rock, grey and brown and green, and sur-

KING EDWARD VII's COFFIN *being carried through the London streets. At the head of the procession walked the new King and his eldest son, the sixteen-year-old Prince of Wales.*

THE DEATH of King Edward VII in May 1910 saw the death also of an era. The years that followed, with his son as King, were to create a new England.

KING GEORGE *with his sons and the Kaiser at the funeral of his father, King Edward VII.*

rounded by evidences of fiery upheavals in the distant past.

Landing is usually effected at Steamer Point ; and here the landing-stage had been converted into a palm-shaded pavilion, whose roof was made up of British flags and whose floor was covered with beautiful eastern carpets. Stretching away from this for five miles to the Crater and the Tanks were triumphal arches and decorations—the palm branches, maize, and millet stalks and ears for which had been brought on camel back from the interior of Yemen.

Along the beach and on either side of the streets in the settlement at Steamer Point and Aden were festoons and scrolls and brightly-coloured lanterns ; while the groups of gaily-clad Arabs, Hindoos, and Comalis, with their beaming, welcoming faces, added not a little to the picturesque effect.

On board the *Ophir*, as she lay off Steamer Point, an impressive ceremony took place before the landing of their Royal Highnesses. Lined up on the deck were those bluejackets and marines of the *Juno* and *St. George* who had served in the South African War, receiving from the Prince the medals which expressed to them their country's appreciation of their valour and steadfastness.

At four o'clock in the afternoon the boat conveying the Duke and Duchess to the landing-stage was seen leaving the side of the *Ophir*, and there broke out to the accompaniment of the saluting guns such cheering from warships and shore as the sunbaked rocks of Aden had never before heard.

European and native seemed to vie with each other in voicing their delight at this visit of the son of the Emperor of India and his gracious consort. On

either side of the pavilion were enclosures filled with European and Asiatic officers and notables and ladies, while drawn up as a guard of honour were the white-uniformed men of the West Kent Regiment, dipping their shot-riddled colours as the Royal visitors passed. Beyond them and around, rising in tiers among the heat-scorched rocks between the settlement and the town, were hundreds of excited Africans and Asiatics, adding their shrill tones to the general hubbub.

Awaiting their Royal Highnesses in the pavilion was the Parsee merchant to whom had been delegated the duty of reading the address of welcome. His father it was who had performed a like function in 1875, when King Edward, then Prince of Wales, landed on the shores of the peninsula. Standing near him were the Sultans of Lahej and Abdali, magnificently clad and attended by their swarthy escort of fierce-looking Arabs.

In a few well-chosen words, spoken in a clear, sonorous voice, the Duke acknowledged and replied to the address ; and then, entering the carriages provided, he and the Duchess drove off to the Tanks, attended by the tall, lithe Bombay Cavalry, and saluted as they passed by the troops guarding the route.

The roads of Aden are splendidly engineered and exceedingly well kept ; and the Royal party rolled along swiftly and pleasantly to the gap in the crags that commands a view of the Crater beyond, with the white-walled town lying in the midst of its grim and forbidding desolation.

Driving through the crowded streets, they arrived at those mighty, walled-up chasms, fifty in number, in which the precious water falling on the bare and rugged hills is stored for the use of townspeople and garrison.

As the evening shadows were falling they returned once more aboard the *Ophir*, where a brilliant reception was held, the people ashore keeping up their rejoicing in the brightly-illuminated streets till the sailing of the *Ophir* just before midnight.

IV

On this particular tour in the Orient liner, India was not visited, being reserved for a future occasion. The course taken was one that, with the exception of Indian harbours and Hong Kong, included all the most considerable distant ports in the Empire.

Ceylon was reached in April, and one of the most interesting incidents of the Duke's stay was the audience which Arabi Pasha was permitted to have with his Royal Highness. At the moment no promise of liberation could be given to the Egyptian ex-rebel, who had been in captivity in Ceylon since his conviction in 1882 ; but his petition was forwarded to London, and no doubt the Duke's accompanying letter was to a large extent the cause of Arabi's release a few months afterwards.

Two days out from Singapore on the way to Melbourne the little fleet crossed the Line and received King Neptune, or rather a series of monarchs who boarded each ship. Prince George had, of course, long ago received his diploma from King Neptune, but he once again volunteered to go through the shaving and christening ceremony.

There was an occasion in later years when Marshal Foch, looking on at the rough but keen regimental games among our armies in France, remarked that the introduction of such sports into the French Army would upset the discipline. It would mean that the colonel would have to take part and win every event.

Continental peoples have always looked askance at such ceremonies as "Crossing the Line," where even a future King of England can be manhandled cheerfully by Neptune and his satellites.

The extreme western point of Australia was seen on April 30. On May 9, the Duke and Duchess began their drive through the gaily-decorated streets of Melbourne. Round the Royal carriages clattered a noble escort drawn from mounted regiments in every State in the Colony and New Zealand. Australia was still on the wave of Boer War enthusiasm, and to do honour to the visitors 1,400 cavalry and 11,000 dismounted troops had been massed in Melbourne, which itself was almost hidden in decorations.

The State opening of Parliament took place on May 9 in the vast building erected at the Centenary Exhibition. The ceremony, well-prepared for, was carried out with perfect dignity.

After the reading of the proclamation summoning the Parliament the Duke, in the King's name, commanded the presence of the members of the House of Representatives who were waiting in an adjoining chamber, and his Royal Highness read the King's commission opening the Parliament.

Of this the most pregnant phrase expressed His Majesty's will " that our said son shall hereby carry to our said Parliament and people our Royal message of goodwill and the assurance of

KING GEORGE AND QUEEN MARY *at the time of their Coronation.*

our earnest prayer for the blessing of Almighty God on the union of our Dominions in Australia in one Federal Commonwealth under the Crown of the United Kingdom of Great Britain and Ireland."

When the Duke had pronounced the words which created a Commonwealth, the Duchess touched with a golden key a golden button and automatically the news was flashed round the world. Twelve thousand voices cheered themselves hoarse, trumpets blared and guns roared defiance. Australia was a united State, subject only to the direct sway of Edward VII.

By a coincidence, while the Duke was inaugurating this Commonwealth Parliament, the Chancellor of the Exchequer in the House of Commons in London was voicing the report of the Committee of Supply that the Duke should have £20,000 a year in addition to the revenue of the Duchy of Cornwall, and that the Duchess should be granted £10,000 a year immediately and £30,000 a year in the unhappy event of widowhood.

While the guns were thundering and the cheers resounding throughout Melbourne, the Prince stepped forward again to read the words of a cablegram he had received from King Edward: " My thoughts are with you on the day of this important event. Most fervently do I wish the Commonwealth of Australia prosperity and great happiness."

At which the cheers broke forth anew. A new nation had been born. A country, almost as large in area as Europe, and with resources as yet hardly tapped, had been brought into being as a member of that Commonwealth of Nations which was to play such an important and dominant part in world history during the next few years. No Roman declaration by a Cæsar could have exceeded in importance this announcement read by a Royal Prince of Britain.

After Melbourne came Queensland. Owing to reported cases of fever, the ships were kept away from Brisbane. The journey was made overland by train, but in order that all things might be done according to plan, the Royal party were taken without ceremony from their railway carriages and, in a Government yacht, landed at Kennedy Wharf.

At Brisbane, 4,000 troops paraded for inspection, and must have congratulated themselves that their own broad-brimmed hats were more suitable to the occasion than the varied military headgear of the suite. The Duke himself was seen to raise his Fusilier headdress more than once to wipe his brow.

Equally enthusiastic scenes marked the reception of the Duke and Duchess in the other State capitals, that at Sydney being particularly noteworthy. Here, as at Melbourne, the crews of the Royal yacht and the escorting vessels enjoyed sixty hours' leave— the first since they left England. On the day after leaving Colombo his Royal Highness intimated by signal his decision on this matter and added a hope that " the men of the Squadron, having a little more money in their pockets than they would have had had they spent it in the great heat of Colombo, will thoroughly enjoy their leave in Australia."

A pleasant musical incident occurred when the degree of LL.D. was conferred on the Duke at the Sydney University. The proceedings, as usual

KING GEORGE'S CORONATION, June 1911. London had never seen before such glittering pageantry as attended their new King's Coronation. 3,000,000 people visited London for the celebrations, and 60,000 troops lined the streets. This photograph shows the impressive scene in Westminster Abbey during the Coronation.

KING GEORGE *in Westminster Abbey during his Coronation.*

THIS PAINTING BY S. SOLOMON *of the banquet following King George's Coronation is the property of the Corporation of London and hangs in the Guildhall. It took the artist eleven years to complete.*

THEIR MAJESTIES KING GEORGE AND QUEEN MARY *in their State robes after the Coronation ceremony.*

on these occasions, were uproarious, and the formalities preceding the presentation of degrees were more or less smothered by the singing of a special " anthem " composed for the occasion. It went to the tune of " A Life on the Ocean Wave," and the chorus ran thus :

Let every man with a voice
His power of lung display ;
Yell loudly and rejoice,
For the Jook is coming to-day ;
The Jook—the Jook—the Jook is coming
to-day,
The Jook—the Jook—the Jook is coming
to-day.

This breezy number amused the " Jook " very much.

And so to New Zealand, one of the farthest-flung to-day of the British Commonwealth of Nations. The visit of Prince George and his wife to New Zealand was marked by an enthusiasm not less than had been shown in Australia. A vast gathering of Maoris assembled for a welcome of their own ; and in the small cities of these islands the splendid fighting material of New Zealand, again to prove itself in the Great War, displayed itself on parade.

None of the cities visited by the Royal party—Auckland, Wellington, Christchurch, or Dunedin—is remarkable for its size or the number of its inhabitants ; for the people of this southern Britain do not crowd together into wildernesses of bricks and mortar, but occupy the land, spreading out over it in thriving little townships and villages and homesteads.

Thousands of them had, however, assembled at Auckland to give to the son of their King and to his consort a hearty and eager welcome, large numbers travelling many miles from remote stations in order to be present when the Duke and Duchess stepped ashore.

As the *Ophir* steamed regally into the beautiful harbour—as beautiful in the opinion of many competent judges as that of Sydney—which opens from the Gulf of Hauraki, attended by the *Juno* and the *St. George*, and passed the six ships of the Australian squadron, " dressed in flags and streamers gay," she was met by a flotilla of steamers, launches, yachts, and sailing-boats bearing welcoming crowds, whose lusty cheers resounded on all sides as she slowly made her way towards the pretty red-roofed town rising in terraces from its long wharves to the wooded slopes of Mount Eden.

Alongside the wharves the water was deep enough for the *Ophir* to lie moored ; and wharves and streets were alike crowded with eager sightseers, many of whom had paid high fees for the privilege of occupying places on the wooden stands whence they might view the procession to Government House. Lining the route were the fine New Zealand soldiery, while the Auckland Mounted Rifles escorted the Royal party and its guard-of-honour of bluejackets.

A feature of the reception, for which their Royal Highnesses expressed their admiration, was a wonderful Union Jack composed of two thousand five hundred schoolchildren dressed in red, white, and blue, a solid column of white-clad youngsters forming the flagstaff.

Leaving Auckland after a most enjoyable stay, the Royal party proceeded to " Windy " Wellington, where there were more interesting functions and presentations of medals.

7

Christchurch, beautifully situated on the verge of the far-famed Canterbury Plains, was the next place at which a prolonged stay was made ; and here a most impressive review of 11,000 New Zealand troops was held in Hagley Park, where also 8,000 schoolchildren sang the National Anthem.

From Christchurch their Royal Highnesses proceeded by train to Dunedin, the thoroughly Scottish capital of the province of Otago, where a welcome as hearty and spontaneous as they had received in any place they had visited was accorded to them. The Prince delighted the citizens by the tone of his reply to the addresses presented to him.

" We have eagerly looked forward," he said, " to visiting this favoured district of New Zealand, knowing that we should find here a community of purely Scottish origin, who some half-century ago left their native shores for this distant land. True to the national inborn capacity for colonisation, they came in whole families under the guidance of trusted leaders, and of their revered minister. They transplanted to their new home in the Southern Seas their national institutions, their characteristic zeal and readiness to make every sacrifice for education. But they did more—they infused into their new life that courage, perseverance, and tenacity of purpose which, together with the spirit of enterprise, are the inherent characteristics of their race. What must then have been but a mere hamlet, but in which they saw with prophetic eye its present greatness, they honoured with the Celtic name of that fairest of cities, the proud historic capital which is the pride of all Scotsmen."

The seventeen days spent in New Zealand had been so pleasant in every way, and the people so warm and cordial in their welcome that it was with regret that their Royal Highnesses sailed from its verdant shores on the night of June 27, and headed through Cook Strait for Hobart in Tasmania.

Then once again the *Ophir* steamed across the Indian Ocean, a fiery, tropical wake swirling at night behind the ship. There was a call at the island of Mauritius, where its French-speaking people displayed their loyalty in an enthusiastic fashion.

Then the little fleet steamed past the island of Réunion, later to become the exile prison of the famous Moroccan chief, Abd-el-Krim, who made a valiant but despairing stand against the forces of France and Spain when those countries extended their sway over Africa.

It was to the great continent of Africa, the sunshine land of the Southern Cross, that the heir to the Throne of England was now travelling.

V

Of all the Dominions visited by the future King George on that first official Empire tour, it may be said that South Africa was to provide the most difficult problem of all.

It might even be added that it is South Africa to-day to which the eyes of the pessimists who predict the downfall of the British Commonwealth of Nations most often turn. Throughout the years of war and struggle between two nations, English and Dutch, south of the Zambesi, statesmanship has done its utmost to make the great experiment of Union possible.

But all those efforts of statesmanship, magnificent though they were and ranging from the declaration of Sir H. Campbell-Bannerman to the whole-hearted support by General Smuts, would have failed utterly if it had not been for the personal presence of royalty.

The first official visit of King George to South Africa, followed many years later by his two sons, the Prince of Wales and the younger Prince George, have all helped to cement that understanding between Briton and Boer, and to call forth that loyalty and affectionate demonstrations to the Throne which have confounded those pessimists who look at this restless Dominion.

At the time the *Ophir* steamed into Durban, the Boer War was not yet over. It was therefore not thought wise that the Duke of York should go up country. Lord Kitchener, however, the masterful military man to whom was given the thankless task of clearing up a spacious sub-continent still smouldering with revolt, came down from Pretoria and welcomed the Duke. There was a meeting in Maritzburg, Natal, and the Duke pinned Victoria Crosses on the breasts of those who had well-earned them in that weary war of the veld.

Later, the *Ophir* steamed towards the Cape and entered the Bay of Simonstown, now the naval headquarters of the South African Squadron.

One episode occurred which was not without significance. A number of Boer prisoners were, by special invitation, present at Admiralty House, Simonstown. The departure of the Duke and Duchess was about to take place, when a deputation drawn from the Boer prisoners presented an address and some specimens of their workmanship. The gifts offered with rugged courtesy were accepted with perfect grace.

Five months earlier Kitchener had written to the War Minister with respect to Louis Botha's refusal to agree to the requirements of Milner and the British Government : " The Boers have a good deal of sentiment of honour, and leaving those, who had helped them, to go to prison for six years would, I feel sure, make it impossible for them to accept the terms offered. We are now carrying on the war to put two or three hundred Dutchmen into prison at the end of it; it seems to me absurd and wrong."

As Sir George Arthur says in his brilliant book : " It was not for the heir to the Crown to traverse in any way the policy of the British Government, however he might agree with the views of the Commander in the field ; but he could—and did—show on August 23, 1901, that what he looked for was not a South Africa beaten to the dust, but eventually a South Africa *amica*, who would harness her energy to England's effort in the day when that effort must be made. Thirteen years later King George would call the Transvaal patriots to battle and range them in line with his own great armies ; the memory of a graceful act had not, perhaps, been wiped from the minds of men who at one time had borne arms against King George's father. . . ."

On August 23 the *Ophir* left South Africa, and by September 14 was making her way up the St. Lawrence, on the way to Quebec. While in this ancient city their Royal Highnesses heard with horror of the assassination of President McKinley, of the United States. From Quebec, the Royal travellers visited Montreal, Ottawa, and Manitoba on their way across the plains to Vancouver. The wide spaciousness, as well as the potential wealth of this great North American Dominion, was revealed to them in a series of striking impressions.

At Calgary, a large body of Red Indians from the Western Reserve had assembled to welcome the grandson of their Great White Mother, a point of view which they insisted that the Duke of Cornwall should not miss. The Party arrived at Vancouver on the 30th and the next day at Victoria was an inspection—of which the Duke appreciated every moment—of the chief British naval base on the Pacific coast of America.

The Falls of Niagara were seen on October 13, and on October 21 the friendly shores of the Dominion were left behind. A brief stay at St. John's enabled the loyalty of the people of Newfoundland to be expressed, and then the *Ophir's* course was set eastwards on the last run of the long cruise.

During the *Ophir* tour the Duke shook hands with thirty-five thousand people, delivered nearly one hundred speeches, and distributed one hundred and forty titles. The brain reels at this endless procession of civic receptions, laying of foundation stones, opening of buildings, and other functions. But the Duke went through it all with a cheery smile and a kind word for everyone.

This particular part of the voyage across the Atlantic was the roughest experienced throughout the whole tour. The bad weather continued even into the English Channel, and the *Ophir* pitched and rolled, causing considerable discomfort even to seasoned sailors.

So high a sea was still running that when King Edward and Queen Alexandra came out on November 1 to meet the squadron, they could not board the *Ophir*, but had to exchange greetings from a steam barge. The landing at Portsmouth was managed that afternoon. Accompanying the King and Queen for this family reunion at Portsmouth was the boy who is now King Edward VIII.

Eight days later, on King Edward's birthday, the Duke was created Prince of Wales and Earl of Chester.

But the real climax of that official Empire tour came with a startling but inspiring speech by the future King George in the heart of London at the Guildhall. It revealed that the tour had made a lasting and splendid impression upon the mind of the Heir to the Throne.

The newly created Prince and Princess of Wales had driven through a lane of cheering crowds to the Guildhall, where they were entertained by the Lord Mayor and Corporation of the City of London. There were many brilliant speeches delivered on that occasion, including one by the Lord Mayor, also by Mr. Joseph Chamberlain, Lord Salisbury, and Lord Rosebery. But it was generally admitted that the reply of the Prince of Wales was the most significant of all.

Replying to the address presented by the City, the Prince of Wales modestly disclaimed the credit of the tour as belonging rather to the King and the Government than to himself. But his concluding words must be quoted at length :

THE INVESTITURE OF THE PRINCE OF WALES AT CARNARVON CASTLE,
*July 13, 1911. He delighted the Welsh people by being the first Prince of Wales ever to
make a speech in the Welsh language.*

"To the distinguished representatives of the commercial interests of the Empire whom I have the pleasure of seeing here to-day, I venture to allude to the impressions which seemed generally to prevail among their brethren across the seas, that the Old Country must wake up if she intends to maintain her old position of pre-eminence in her Colonial trade against foreign competitors.

"No one who had the privilege of enjoying the experiences which we have had during the tour could fail to be struck with one all-prevailing and pressing want—the want of population. Even in the oldest of our Colonies there were abundant signs of this need. Boundless tracts of country are yet unexplored, hidden mineral wealth calling for development, vast expanses of virgin soil ready to yield profitable crops to the settlers. And these can be enjoyed under conditions of healthy living, liberal laws, free institutions, in exchange for the overcrowded cities and the almost hopeless struggle for existence which, alas! too often is the lot of many in the Old Country.

"But one condition, and one only, is made by our Colonial brethren, and that is, 'Send us suitable emigrants.' I would go farther, and appeal to my fellow-countrymen at home to prove the strength of the attachment of the Motherland to her children by sending to them only her best. By this means we may still further strengthen, or at all events pass on unimpaired, that pride of race, that unity of sentiment and purpose, that feeling of common loyalty and obligation which knit together and alone can maintain the integrity of our Empire."

"Wake Up, England!" The speech rang through the Empire. It was hailed as an omen of the happiest augury that the future King should have so clear a view of the nation's needs and should express himself so boldly and stirringly about them. He was revealed a man of vision. It came as a surprise to many.

But that faculty for surprising people King George kept up to the very end of his busy life. What people had come to regard as the figurehead of the British Constitution spoke on occasions very wisely, shrewdly, and to the point. The shock to many was as though the Sphinx had made utterance. Too often, King George had been underestimated. And his own innate modesty often let that underestimation go unchallenged.

The "Wake Up England" speech shook the nation out of its complacency. Even statesmen began to eye this Prince of the outspoken utterance with a new and somewhat puzzled regard.

VI

From now on the Prince of Wales took up with a will the hard work which is expected from the heir to a constitutional throne. This work became harder even than usual, and far more anxious when King Edward fell ill on the eve of his Coronation.

Now were revealed the Prince's powers of organisation, his sailor-like determination to have everything done in an orderly and shipshape way. He gave a clear indication of the service he would expect when he became King, and, of course, the experience was very useful to him.

When he was preparing for his own

KING GEORGE AND QUEEN MARY, *photographed at the Viceregal Lodge, Dublin, in* 1911.

Coronation, it was said by one who visited Buckingham Palace that King George " ran it as if it were a man-of-war." He was a firm believer in the old adage " A place for everything and everything in its place." He could get through a mass of work far more pleasantly than most men, simply because he had followed a wise method and would never be either hurried or delayed.

Ceremonies of various kinds in the United Kingdom, with occasional visits to France and Germany, uneventfully filled up the next few years. Life at Marlborough House, at York Cottage, Sandringham, and at Frogmore, in Windsor Forest, flowed on happily. The children were a constant delight to their father as well as to the Princess of Wales.

They grew up admirably trained, with charming manners. One morning in Windsor Park two of the little princes were riding with their father, and in the excitement of a good canter on the turf forgot to acknowledge the lifted hats of some labourers by the roadside.

At once the Prince wheeled them back, and next moment the astonished working men received the most elaborate salutes from the two small boys, with prettily murmured apologies for their want of courtesy.

The Prince and Princess of Wales had six children born to them, five sons and one daughter. Of these, the Prince of Wales, who now ascends the Throne —known in the intimacy of his parents' home as " David "—was born on June 23, 1894 ; Prince Albert (the Duke of York) was born on December 14, 1895 ; and on April 25, 1897, Princess Mary (the Countess of Harewood),

Prince Henry (the Duke of Gloucester), Prince George, and Prince John (who died in 1919) appeared during the early years of this century.

King George was a first-rate shot, one of the best in England, and he never let slip an opportunity of enlarging his experience. When he was in Canada there was a good deal of scepticism about his really being exceptionally skilful with his gun.

This lasted until he was asked to go shooting prairie-hens. Of course, he found these perfectly easy to hit ; in fact, he bagged every one that rose. After a while a member of his suite heard one Canadian whisper to another, " Say, if they don't move this Prince on soon, there won't be a prairie-hen left in the country."

The Coronation of King Edward VII, after its postponement in consequence of the King's illness, threw a great deal of work on the shoulders of the Prince of Wales, who had to entertain the distinguished guests assembled for the auspicious occasion. He held a review of the Colonial troops on the Horse Guards' Parade on July 1, 1902, when the Indian and foreign Princes were present. During 1903, he inaugurated, on May 15, the first section of the London County Council's electric tramways, visited the American squadron at Portsmouth, and was present, with the Princess at the launch of the warship *King Edward VII*, at Plymouth.

During the next few years, apart from the many State functions in which he took a more or less prominent part, Prince George enjoyed a well-earned rest, interesting himself very deeply in agricultural questions. He became deservedly well known in agricultural

KING GEORGE *rode into Delhi for the Durbar in December* 1911 *amid scenes of great rejoicing.
It was announced by the King at the Durbar that the capital of India was to be Delhi
and not* Calcutta.

KING GEORGE AND QUEEN MARY *wore their crowns and Coronation robes, and were surrounded by the leading princes of India.*

DELHI DURBAR, 1911. 80,000 *troops and civilians were present at this great pageant.* *A remarkable incident followed the ceremony, when 200,000 people filed past the throne on which the King Emperor had sat.*

MORE SCENES AT THE DURBAR, *where the pageantry of India was displayed before the King Emperor.*

circles for his breed of red poll cattle, and for a strain of Berkshire pigs, showing points of excellence not before produced in those very useful animals.

But the Empire was again clamouring for the Prince to resume his journeys. Above all, India, which had been excluded from the first official Empire tour. Arrangements were now made for the Prince of Wales to visit this great Eastern dependency. In October 1905, the Prince and Princess sailed for India upon a tour that was to last some five months.

Their vessel, H.M.S. *Renown*, reached Bombay on November 9, the coincidence of King Edward's birthday being noted and welcomed throughout India as an augury of good fortune. The welcome to the Prince of Wales in Bombay was warm and unmistakable.

He was greeted by the Viceroy, Lord Curzon, and after a stay of four or five days in Bombay, the Prince and Princess proceeded to Indore, where the Central Indian chiefs, including that most interesting of Eastern women, the late Begum of Bhopal, were gathered to welcome them.

At Jaipur, the picturesque Maharaja welcomed the Prince with touching fervour. Here his Royal Highness, like his father before him, shot his first tiger.

A certain feature marked this journey which had never before been attempted, even in romantic India. Their Royal Highnesses left Rangoon in the later afternoon, and as evening fell it was seen that the train ran through a veritable avenue of fire. On each side of the track stood silent Burmese torchbearers, three to every furlong, and until dawn broke again in the East the succeeding wisps of red flame flashed a fiery welcome.

From Rangoon to Mandalay the Prince and Princess had a 385-miles railway journey. The Burma Railway has a metre gauge with carriages rather too wide in proportion, and the train rocks badly at any speed of more than twenty miles an hour.

" Nineteen hours for three hundred and eighty miles ! " exclaimed the Prince. " No, no. You must cut the time down by at least half."

It was an Imperial command. The train set off. There were indescribable scenes as it rocketed and bucked along the narrow-gauge lines, but Mandalay was reached—ten hours ahead of schedule. The Prince and Princess descended looking sadly travel-worn, and the first use to which the Prince put his speech when he regained it, was to express his opinion of the Burma Railway in round terms.

The tour in India may pale in importance and glory beside the great occasion of the Coronation Durbar. But if a certain sameness marked the proceedings at the various places visited, if receptions by local officials and notables and presentations of loyal addresses tend to monotony, both Prince and Princess undoubtedly enjoyed to the full what was the glorious spectacle of Oriental pageantry. They sailed from Karachi for England on March 17.

On their return the Prince, at the Guildhall, on May 17, again gave an account of his tour. Recalling his former visit to " our sister nations beyond the seas," he pointed out that the conclusion of his visit to the Indian Empire might be regarded as the completion of the mission originally entrusted to him by the King.

In India, he said, although he and the Princess had been welcomed everywhere by holiday-making crowds, they did not forget the misery and poverty which existed in the famine districts through which they passed. He had been impressed by the loyalty and personal allegiance to the Crown of the great feudatory Princes, their nobility of mind, and the great powers which they possessed for doing good. He described the Imperial Service troops raised by these Princes and destined, ten years later, to play a gallant part in the World War. Finally, he spoke of the wonderful administration of India, with its population of 300,000,000 of diverse races, languages and creeds, and many grades of civilisation, and revealed his insight into a grave problem in the words :

" I cannot help thinking from all I have heard and seen that the task of governing India will be made the easier if we, on our part, infuse into it a wider element of sympathy. I will venture to predict that to such sympathy there will be an ever-abundant and genuine response. May we not also hope for a still fuller measure of trust and confidence in our earnest desire and efforts to promote the well-being and to further the best interests of every class ? "

That was a kingly utterance, the utterance of one who felt himself called upon to lead. It had its effect both in India and at home.

When King George announced his resolve to be crowned in person at the Coronation Durbar, all who had good memories or who knew His Majesty's intimate feelings saw in this only a further proof of his affection for the Dependency which gave to British Sovereigns their Imperial title, and his anxiety to prove to its peoples the goodwill and sympathetic interest of the British race.

VII

It was in this same year that the Prince of Wales found himself in the midst of a European event which was, in itself, a foreshadowing of those terrible times when war would stalk the land and European thrones topple over in the dust of revolution.

While in India, the Prince of Wales had been told of the betrothal of Princess Ena of Battenburg to King Alfonso of Spain. The necessary change in his cousin's religion had aroused a good deal of disapproval among Protestants in Britain. Nevertheless, the Royal marriage was fixed, and the future King George and Queen Mary were to represent this country at the wedding.

The Prince and Princess of Wales— accompanied by Prince and Princess Alexander of Teck—made a hot and rather uncomfortable journey to Madrid for the wedding, which took place on May 31. This was the occasion when a dastardly attempt was made to assassinate King Alfonso and Queen Ena.

As the bridal pair were returning to the Palace from the Church at San Geronimo, an anarchist flung a bomb at the Royal carriage, several soldiers and spectators being killed, while the assassin committed suicide to avoid arrest.

The bravery of the bride at once gained for her the intense respect, to deepen quickly into affection, of the Spanish people. Her wedding dress

KING GEORGE *on a big-game hunting expedition in India.*

splashed with blood, she appeared quite unmoved, and the only anxiety and emotion she expressed was on behalf of the killed and injured. To the Prince and Princess of Wales in that procession, the attempted assassination must have caused some deep misgivings as to the future of the Spanish monarchy.

Some time before the celebration of his Silver Jubilee, King George and Queen Mary were to receive in England that same royal couple whose wedding they had attended. This time, Alfonso and Ena were the exiles of a Spanish revolution.

Throughout the turbulent years, King Alfonso, helped staunchly by Queen Ena, had made a gallant and brave stand against the subversive forces of the country. The King's gesture was, indeed, such a splendid one that it earned the respect of the revolutionaries and no doubt helped considerably in enabling the Royal Family of Spain to escape with their lives intact.

Three months at home, and then the Prince was off again, representing King Edward at the Tercentennial Celebrations at Quebec in July 1908. He was received with tremendous enthusiasm by the Canadian people, and presented to Earl Grey, the Governor-General, the sum of £90,000, subscribed by British citizens in all parts of the Empire and American sympathisers for the acquisition of the battlefields of Quebec for the people of the Dominion.

Carrying a present from Nova Scotians to the Princess—it was a beautiful fur cloak of mink skin with buttons of 24-carat Nova Scotia gold—the Prince made the return voyage in the *Indomitable*, which steamed across the Atlantic at an average speed of 24·8 knots. The war vessel's performance was regarded as a remarkable one, and the nation was interested to learn a few days after her arrival that the Prince himself had taken a turn in the stokehold, throwing into the furnaces six shovelfuls of coal "for luck."

Between the end of 1908 and his accession in May 1910, the Prince of Wales quietly carried out the manifold duties devolving on the Heir to the Throne, now laying a foundation-stone or opening an infirmary ; now presiding at the meeting of some charitable organisation, or attending other public gatherings.

During the sittings of Parliament he was often in his place on the cross-benches of the House of Lords, and when important debates were in progress in the House of Commons he was occasionally to be seen looking down from the place always reserved for him behind the clock.

It was during this period that, despite his devotion to his own children, the future King George revealed that kindly, fatherly interest in all young people. An intimate glimpse of this side of the King's life was broadcast after his death by Mr. O. F. Morshead, librarian at Windsor Castle.

"King George," he said, "loved children, as the greatest men so often do ; and so I will try to tell about some of the fine personal characteristics which underlay the robes and trappings of State. Every year he used to give a prize to some selected candidate from one of the local schools ; and if one of those boys or girls were here at the microphone now instead of me, this is the account he could give you. He would say :

A GREAT NAVAL REVIEW *was held just before the war, and was attended by King George and the Prince of Wales.*

SUFFRAGETTE INTERFERES WITH THE DERBY. Miss Emily Davison threw herself in front of King George's horse Anmer during the 1913 Derby, just as the horses were rounding Tattenham Corner. The woman died from her injuries four days later. Both the horse and jockey were injured.

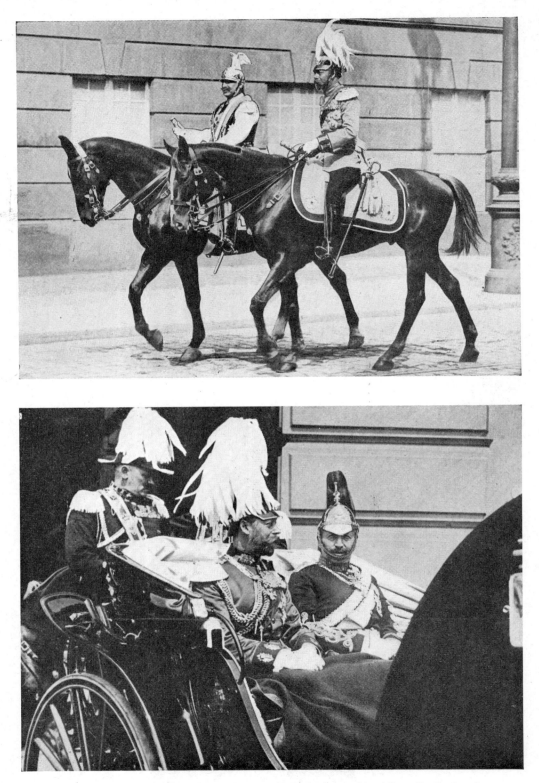

KING GEORGE WITH THE GERMAN EMPEROR *during his visit to Berlin for the marriage of the Kaiser's daughter to the Duke of Brunswick.*

IN THE ROBES *of a Knight of St. Patrick.*

THE FAMOUS ROYAL BARGE. *The top photograph shows it during a procession on the Thames, and the latter was taken during a Royal visit to Henley.*

" ' I was shown up into the King's study, quite a small room, and there was the King standing on the hearth-rug, and shaking hands with me and talking just as if he had known me all my life. I was ever so frightened before I went in, but the funny thing was that, directly he started talking I felt as if I'd known him all my life.

" ' He asked me all about home and whether any of our people were out of work and whether I was as proud of being a Norfolk person as he was, and a whole lot of other things ; and it seemed all the time as if he really wanted to know.

" ' And while I was talking I looked round at the rather hard-looking leather chairs ; and the grey parrot on the stand, which seemed fond of him ; and the little dog which was looking at him ; and the neat pile of books on the low table by his chairs ; and a lot of scarlet dispatch-boxes— one of them was open and a great big paper was lying on it which he had been reading when I came in.

" ' Presently he took up a Bible, saying that that was what he was going to give me ; but before doing that he wanted to tell me a story. " When I was your age," he said, " my grand-mother (she was Queen Victoria, you know) gave me a Bible, and she advised me to read a chapter in it every night. I have always done it, wherever I have been—except, of course, during that bad illness ; I couldn't do it then. Now you can do as you like, but if you make that a rule of your life, and stick to it, I don't think you'll regret it when you come to my age . . . and you've got a long way to go yet." ' "

That story, said Mr. Morshead, was true. King George was, at whatever angle one met him, a profoundly honest man. He was only proud of two things : of the antiquity of his kingly office and of his birthright as an Englishman.

In the spring of 1910 all the plans had been laid for a tour through South Africa on the occasion of the opening of the first Union Parliament. But a more burdensome task was in store for the Prince.

On the night of May 6, 1910, King Edward died and his son suc-ceeded to the Throne.

CHAPTER IV

GEORGE ASCENDS THE THRONE

King Edward VII's Last Hours—The Accession Speech—Coronation Scenes in London—What the Kaiser said—Investiture of the Prince of Wales at Carnarvon Castle—The King and Queen visit India—The Delhi Durbar—The World prepares for War.

I

THE death of King Edward VII marked the end of another epoch in the history of the Empire. "Edwardian" that period was called, and maybe the term will be again in fashion with the accession of Edward VIII. But the period during which the future King George learned his kingship and the arts of ruling a great Empire was an important one.

The death of Edward VII was a sudden and dramatic one. It has been told in a companion volume, *The Story of Twenty-five Years*. It is a story worth retelling for all the implications it possessed upon the reign of the new King George V.

A grey-bearded man sat at a tea-table in a room in Buckingham Palace. He looked tired and ill. From his chair he could see the bright green of lawn and trees shaded by the sunshine of a May afternoon.

Fumbling for a cigar, he put it between his lips and lit it with an air of finality. But he had only taken a few puffs when he was seized with a paroxysm of coughing. Large brown patches appeared on the familiar face. His hands trembled.

The door opened quietly. A frock-coated medical man approached the coughing figure.

" Your Majesty ! " he begged. " These cigars . . ."

Britain's greatest diplomat, King Edward VII, gazed with tear-dimmed eyes, brought on by the coughing, at his medical attendant and tried to wave him away. But the medical man had glimpsed something else. By the tea-table was a mass of official documents that the King had been perusing.

" Your Majesty," he again pleaded, " I implore you to rest."

With an effort King Edward recovered his breath.

" No, no," he wheezed, shaking his head. " I shall work to the end. . . . Of what use is it to be alive if one cannot work ? "

The medical man shrugged his shoulders. A gesture from the King and he withdrew. But no sooner had the door closed than the grey-bearded man, clutching the cigar between his fingers, was once again doubled by a fit of coughing.

This time it was a good four minutes before he recovered. He breathed noisily and painfully.

" If this lasts much longer," he muttered to himself, " I am done for."

An hour later he was receiving a high colonial official and discussing with an effort matters of State. As the official left Buckingham Palace, he was

BRITAIN AT WAR. *Thousands gathered outside Buckingham Palace when war was declared to demonstrate their loyalty to their Sovereign. Within a few hours Sir John French had assumed control of the Army, and Sir John Jellicoe of the Navy, and the nation began a war that was to last over four years. Yet in August 1914 most people* **expected it to be over by Christmas.**

KING GEORGE IN FRANCE. *A war-time photograph.*

KING GEORGE *asking a few questions about gas-bombs* **during** *a visit to the Front.*

heard to remark : " I have seen a dying man."

Meanwhile, in another room of the Palace, other medical men had gathered. A Cabinet Minister. Also the King's Private Secretary. It was still the tradition of Britain that the illness of royalty should, unless terribly serious, be kept secret from the public. At the same time it was decided to send an urgent telegram to Queen Alexandra, who was at Corfu.

" It is best that the Queen returns at once," decided the doctors.

Hurriedly the Private Secretary composed a telegram, and, by means of official channels, it was flashed towards that island in the Mediterranean.

On the morning of May 6, 1910, the doctors examined King Edward. He was very ill. The heart was failing. Yet the King was ominously calm. He refused to stay in bed. He dressed himself fully, and sat again in that room overlooking the Palace Gardens. At one period he walked painfully to the other side of the Palace and looked down towards the Mall. A criss-cross of scaffolding and grey tarpaulin covered the huge mass that was to be a monument to Queen Victoria, a work in progress.

" I shall never live to see it unveiled," he nodded, a strange smile hiding itself beneath the beard as he thought of that great mother Queen who had chided him as Prince of Wales for his glittering, rather feverish, life.

What was it they had said to him ? The dying man struggled to recall the whispers of those about him.

" . . . He likes the society of women who can talk, of Jews, and people who can amuse him. And he really likes any public ceremony, and theatres and cards. . . . But he is a sensible man, and knows more about foreign affairs than anyone, and has quite advanced ideas. . . ."

King Edward chuckled. Yes, he had lived his period. Edwardian, they would call it. And many would look back upon it with regret. Few realised at the time that in their dying King was England at her zenith, her richest and most powerful. Even then the clouds were gathering on the horizon. And he, Edward, shrewdest of all the diplomats, had glimpsed them. His many journeys to the Continent had been in the nature of a preparation for the storm.

With a sigh, King Edward wandered back to his sitting-room. He tried to smoke another cigar, but got no pleasure from it.

" I feel miserably ill," he confessed, laying the cigar aside.

At eleven o'clock he wanted to rise to receive his old friend, Sir Ernest Cassel, who found him in his sitting-room, dressed as usual. The King rose from his arm-chair to shake Cassel's hand, but looked as if he had suffered, and could not speak distinctly. But he still had his kindly smile.

" I am very ill," he murmured, " but I wanted to see you. . . ."

Once again in that other room the medical men had met. This time a public bulletin had to be issued. At the same time the Archbishop of Canterbury was summoned. Rumours began to be whispered through the streets of London. The King was dying ; the King was dead. . . .

In the official residence of the Prime Minister, 10 Downing Street, Mrs. Asquith was handing a telegram to a servant. It was addressed to her husband, urging him to return at once. Even as the servant padded away, Lord Kitchener was announced. He entered the room.

"Have you heard the dreadful rumour?" whispered Mrs. Asquith.

Lord Kitchener jerked his head impatiently.

"Absurd!" he snapped. "You've only to look out of the window. The flag on the Palace isn't at half-mast yet."

And, indeed, the Royal Standard was still flying in the windy May sunshine.

The serious bulletin published at eleven o'clock cast a gloom over the luncheon tables of the West End. At Kempton Park a huge crowd of race-goers anxiously watched the board go up for the 4.15 race. The King's horse, Witch, was scheduled to run. Would it be scratched at the last moment? But a cheer was raised when it was seen that the horse would run after all. And even greater and prolonged cheering greeted the finish of the race with Witch an easy winner. It was considered a happy omen.

Inside Buckingham Palace, the Prince of Wales received the glad news and hurried into the sitting-room to congratulate his father.

The grey-bearded figure nodded, and tried to smile.

"Yes, they told me . . . I am glad."

A few moments later he slipped into a coma. Queen Alexandra, who had returned from Corfu, herself helped to carry him to his bedroom. He was undressed and laid on the bed.

"I will go on . . . I will go on . . ." he muttered determinedly.

But they were the last coherent words King Edward spoke. Even whilst he was still struggling against death, a Privy Council had been summoned to proclaim his successor. And, in accordance with tradition, a regiment of Life Guards stood by, booted and spurred, ready for emergencies.

Groups of people began to drift towards the Palace. They clustered the railings and stared silently at those lighted windows where a King was fighting his last desperate battle. Some shivered in the cool night air. A woman wrapped a shawl round her baby. Dumb faces stared upwards.

At a quarter to twelve King Edward breathed his last. A member of the Royal Household came down and stepped across the gravel to the railings. His feet crunched nearer and nearer, a messenger of ill-tidings.

He faced the crowd through the railings.

"The King is dead," he said quietly.

A deep silence fell on the crowd. Men fumbled for their hats and removed them. A woman's sob seemed to shake them. The news, though not unexpected, was stunning.

"The King is dead."

That quiet announcement was already flaring and resounding throughout the world. Mr. Asquith, the Prime Minister, at the moment aboard the Admiralty yacht *Enchantress*, pitching full-steam ahead from the Mediterranean to England, received the news at three o'clock in the morning. He rose from his bunk and went on deck.

Above the pitching mast in the pale glow of the dawn, Halley's comet blazed across the sky.

"The King is dead; long live the King!"

King George V had begun his reign.

KING GEORGE WITH MARSHAL FOCH.

KING GEORGE INSPECTING THE FRONT, *wearing a tin helmet as a precaution against shell-fire.*

KING GEORGE *at the front with the King of the Belgians.*

KING GEORGE *with President Poincaré and Sir Douglas Haig.*

KING GEORGE *among his troops.*

II

At half-past four the following afternoon, one hundred and fifty Privy Councillors met in the large hall at St. James's Palace. A silent, hushed assembly. No greetings, no handshakes.

Lord Crewe rose from his seat. A strange, tense silence held all who were present.

"The King is dead," announced Lord Crewe simply, "and it is our duty to proclaim his successor."

The Lord Chancellor and the Archbishop of Canterbury then went out of the room. In a few moments they returned. Walking between them was the Prince of Wales, whom Lord Crewe presented to the Council as King George V. After a few words the King took his seat on the throne and all those present knelt before him on a cushion, swearing their loyalty, each in the manner of his faith.

That same evening Mrs. Asquith dined with Winston Churchill and Lord and Lady Crewe. After dinner Churchill rose, and, holding his glass on high, said : "Let us drink to the health of the new King." And Lord Crewe replied : "Or, rather, to the memory of the old."

The black velvet darkness of night was over England. In the Throne Room at Buckingham Palace, four Grenadier Guardsmen, their heads bowed over their reversed rifles, stood at the corners of the coffin in a long, silent vigil. . . .

At nine o'clock on the morning of May 9, 1910, an ancient and picturesque ceremonial was unrolled. A Guard of Honour of the First Life Guards clattered into Friary Court of the Palace, followed by the band of the Coldstream Guards with draped guns. Behind them rode the Army Headquarters staff in full-dress uniform. The red- and blue-garbed figures stood out against the grey stone background of the Palace.

A great crowd assembled for the ceremony. A fanfare of trumpets drew all eyes to the balcony overlooking the quadrangle. The State trumpeters had raised their shining instruments. Figures in colourful robes and uniforms stalked on to the balcony. The group included the Duke of Norfolk, Earl Marshal, and Garter King-of-Arms, and Pursuivants of the Heralds' College.

From a window of Marlborough House, opposite the quadrangle, three young boys and a girl watched this picturesque ceremonial. They were the children of King George. At another window, though unseen by the people, were the King and Queen.

After that preliminary fanfare of trumpets, there was silence for a few moments. Then the Garter King-of-Arms stepped forward, unrolled a scroll, and began to read in a loud, clear voice :

". . . Whereas it has pleased Almighty God to call to His Mercy our late Sovereign Lord King Edward the Seventh, of Blessed and Glorious Memory, by whose Decree the Imperial Crown of the United Kingdom of Great Britain and Ireland is solely and rightfully come to the High and Mighty Prince George Frederick Ernest Albert :

"We, therefore, the Lords Spiritual and Temporal of this Realm being here assisted with those of His late Majesty's Privy Council, with numbers of other principal gentlemen of quality, with the Lord Mayor, Aldermen and citizens of

London, do now hereby, with one voice and content of tongue and heart, publish and proclaim :

" That the High and Mighty Prince George Frederick Ernest Albert is now, by the death of our late Sovereign of happy memory, become our only lawful right Liege Lord George the Fifth by the Grace of God King of the United Kingdom of Great Britain and Ireland, and of the British Dominions beyond the Seas, Defender of the Faith, Emperor of India, to whom we do acknowledge all faith and constant obedience, with all hearty and humble affection, beseeching God, by whom Kings and Queens do reign, to bless the Royal Prince George the Fifth with long and happy years to reign over us. . . ."

As the clear voice of the reader of the proclamation rang out, the troops stood at the salute and the men in the large crowd bared their heads. When the voice of the Garter King-of-Arms ceased there was a breathless silence. Then the Earl Marshal raised his gloved hand.

" God Save the King ! " he cried.

III

Rarely has a monarch been faced with such a confused national situation as confronted King George V at his accession. The first few months of his reign were to tax all the wisdom and resources of his statecraft.

The Archbishop of Canterbury, preaching in St. Paul's Cathedral a quarter of a century later at that ever-memorable Silver Jubilee Thanksgiving, truly said that more perhaps than in any previous period in our history these twenty-five years had been " years of almost unbroken anxiety and strain."

At the start there was trouble and unrest everywhere. Foreign affairs were in a disturbed state. In Britain itself a grave Constitutional crisis was impending.

At his first Privy Council, King George, who was then approaching his forty-fifth year, created an excellent impression. Mr. Asquith was " deeply moved by his modesty and good sense " ; Sir Edward Grey was " touched by the profound sorrow with which he spoke of the bereavement."

The Accession Speech, spoken by King George, is well worth giving in full. It was the forerunner of many deep, emotional speeches that the King made to his people, culminating in that final Christmas broadcast of 1935.

" My Lords and gentlemen, my heart is too full for me to address you to-day in more than a few words. It is my sorrowful duty to announce to you the death of my dearly-beloved Father, the King. In this irreparable loss which has so suddenly fallen upon me and upon the whole Empire, I am comforted by the feeling that I have the sympathy of my future subjects, who will mourn with me for their beloved sovereign whose own happiness was found in sharing and promoting theirs. I have lost not only a father's love, but the affectionate and intimate relations of a dear friend and adviser. No less confident am I in the universal loving sympathy which is assured to my dearest Mother in her overwhelming grief.

KING GEORGE *paid several visits to the Front, where he decorated soldiers for their bravery.*

KING GEORGE AND THE PRINCE OF WALES *inspecting R.F.C. aeroplanes.*

KING GEORGE AND QUEEN MARY *inspecting W.A.A.C.'s (Women's Auxiliary Army Corps) at Aldershot. They were recruited to work behind the lines.*

" Standing here a little more than nine years ago, our beloved King declared that as long as there was breath in his body he would work for the good and amelioration of his people. I am sure that the opinion of the whole nation will be that this declaration has been fully carried out.

" To endeavour to follow in his footsteps, and at the same time to uphold the constitutional government of these realms, will be the earnest object of my life. I am deeply sensible of the very heavy responsibilities which have fallen upon me. I know that I can rely on Parliament and upon the people of these Islands and of my Dominions beyond the seas for their help in the discharge of these arduous duties, and for their prayers that God will grant me strength and guidance. I am encouraged by the knowledge that I have in my dear wife one who will be a constant helpmate in every endeavour for our people's good."

Fifteen days later, the King issued his first message to the people of Britain.

" The voice of affection and of loving devotion to the memory of my dear Father which has come from every part of the Empire, the outward public demonstrations, especially those in the Capital during the two stages of his passing to his last resting-place, and the pathetic manner in which vast multitudes of his loving subjects patiently and reverently awaited opportunity to pay a last tribute to his memory, have profoundly touched me and my whole Family.

" A sorrow so sudden and unlooked-for might well have been overwhelming. But the sentiments evoked by it have made me realise that it is a loss common to me and my people ; they share it with me. I do not stand alone.

" With such thoughts I take courage, and hopefully look into the future ; strong in my faith in God, trusting my people, and cherishing the Laws and Constitution of my beloved Country."

Nor was the Empire forgotten in the King's grateful thanks. In a special message from Marlborough House, dated the same day and addressed " To my People beyond the Seas," he wrote :

" The innumerable messages of kindness from my loyal subjects beyond the Seas have deeply touched my heart, and have assured me that I have in full measure their sympathy in the great trial which has befallen me and them, that my sorrow is their sorrow, that we share a common loss.

" The happiness of all his people throughout his dominions was dear to the heart of my beloved Father. For them he lived and worked, in their service he died, and I cannot doubt that they will hold his name in grateful remembrance. I am now called to follow in his footsteps and carry on the work which prospered in his hands.

" As a sailor I have been brought into constant touch with the overseas dominions of the Crown, and I have personally realised the affectionate loyalty which holds together many lands and diverse peoples in one glorious fellowship.

" Nine years ago I travelled through the Empire, accompanied by my dear wife, and, had the late King lived, we should together, at his express wish, have visited South Africa in the coming

KING GEORGE WITH EARL BEATTY.

PRESENTING DECORATIONS _to officers in the Royal Navy._

KING GEORGE *paying a war-time visit to his Fleet.*

Autumn, to open the First Parliament of the South African Union, the latest and greatest evidence of that peace and harmony which my Father ever loved to promote.

"It will be my earnest endeavour to uphold constitutional government and to safeguard in all their fullness the liberties which are enjoyed throughout my dominions, and, under the good guidance of the Ruler of all men, I will maintain upon the foundation of freedom, justice and peace the great heritage of the United British Empire."

The references to "the constitutional government of these realms" had a deeper significance than could have been attached to the pledge which is usually given on accession to the Throne. A constitutional crisis was, in fact, existing. To understand the situation as it existed at the death of King Edward, it is necessary to go back a few months. It will be remembered that the closing months of his life had witnessed a more bitter struggle between the two Houses of Parliament than had been known for centuries. The Radical party had for years complained that the House of Lords acted as a perpetual obstacle to the huge programme of legislation to which the Liberal successors of Mr. Gladstone were helplessly committed.

Their grievances were based on principle rather than upon practice. They contended that the constitution of the House of Lords was an anachronism, and that its absolute power of veto must be curtailed. The first point was in fact admitted by the Lords.

It was over the second contention that matters came to a crisis, on November 30, 1909, when Mr. Lloyd George's Budget was rejected by the House of Lords. No better battlefield could have been wished by the Radicals. The legal right of the House of Lords to interfere in national finance was not denied, but even on the Conservative side there were not wanting those who said it was unconstitutional.

The immediate result of this rejection was an appeal to the country. In January 1910, in the course of a bitterly contested struggle, the Government lost about 100 seats. They still, however, commanded a majority in the House so long as they received the support of the Irish party, the total majority of Liberals, Irish, and Socialist members together over the Unionists being 124.

Although the number of Conservatives and Liberals was practically identical, Mr. Asquith—as the late Lord Oxford and Asquith then was—contended that he had received a mandate to carry out a drastic scheme of reforming the House of Lords.

But in 1910 the House of Lords passed the Budget without demur. As the people had been directly consulted on it, the Peers claimed no constitutional right to interfere a second time. They also took into consideration Lord Rosebery's proposals for the reform of the constitution and powers of their House. This, however, was the last thing that Mr. Asquith wished. He intended to hamstring the Upper House; and he naturally preferred that the Second Chamber should not, by a process of self-purgation, increase its prestige and political importance.

The Conservatives, besides recognising the difficulty in which the new King was placed, had everything to gain by delay. Even the Irish and Socialist parties felt that the situation was one

WOUNDED SOLDIERS *visiting Buckingham Palace for a tea-party.*

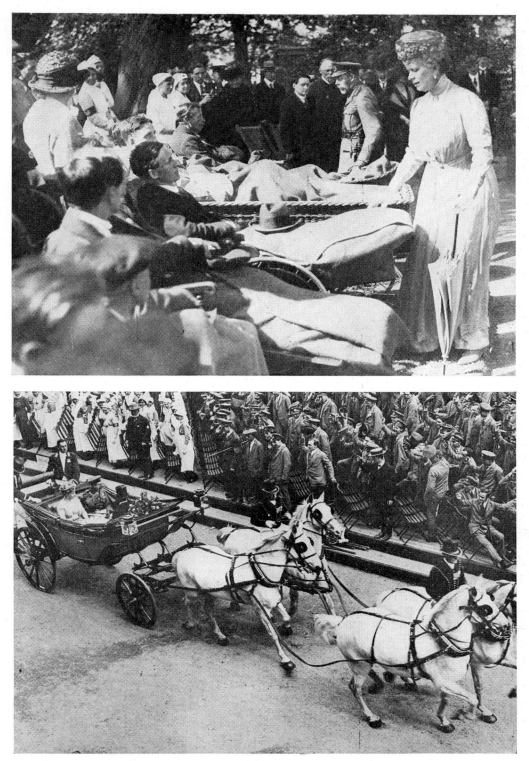

KING GEORGE AND QUEEN MARY *among the soldiers wounded in the War.*

that King George, until he had time and opportunity for consultation and consideration, could not with fairness be asked to face. For nearly six months, therefore, an armed neutrality reigned in British politics.

The Irish held the scales, and their refusal to be contented with anything less than the practical destruction of the power of veto possessed by the House of Lords foredoomed peace efforts to failure.

The new Sovereign had learned from his father a wide political toleration, and a determination to uphold by every means in his power the strict constitutional attitude which the British nation has come to expect of its Monarch. But in this case the Constitution itself was at stake.

The proposal of the Government, indeed, had for its aim something hardly distinguishable from Single-Chamber government, and the delicate question arose as to the extent to which a Sovereign bound by oath to uphold the existing Constitution could assent to a movement which practically had the effect of destroying it.

Feeling was running high in the country. Though the majority of the electors were in no position to estimate aright the importance or the trend of the issues involved, the Government had, as a matter of fact, made an appeal to them, and the country had given Mr. Asquith a majority. No detailed scheme of reform, however, had in January 1910 been produced. A large section of the Ministerial supporters clamoured for immediate action.

What was meant was nothing less than this : Mr. Asquith even before the December election, armed by the result of the January contest, was to re-quest the new King to give him a private assurance that, failing all other means, the programme of the Radicals should be carried out by the intervention of the King himself. He was to undertake, if necessary, to create a sufficient number of peers—500 was the number suggested—to bear down the opposition of the House of Lords to the Government's proposal.

The second election of 1910 merely confirmed the previous decision of the country. The new Parliament was formally opened by the King on February 6.

The most exciting Constitutional struggle since the first Reform Bill then began. The Government brought in and passed their Parliament Bill by the middle of May. The House of Lords gave it a second reading, and then, after a brief suspension of the conflict for the Coronation, completely transformed it in Committee by substituting the Referendum for the Suspensory Veto.

The crisis followed swiftly. For as the " contingency " for which the Government had obtained before the election a provisional assurance from the King had then clearly arisen, the Cabinet submitted to the King a Minute, published by the late Lord Oxford in his *Fifty Years of Parliament*, which contained the following passage :

" Parliament having been twice dissolved during the last eighteen months and the future relations between the two Houses having been at both elections a predominant issue, a third dissolution is wholly out of the question.

" Hence, in the contingency contemplated, it will be the duty of Ministers to advise the Crown to exer-

ONE OF KING GEORGE'S MOST FAMOUS PHOTOGRAPHS. *It shows him talking to a little war-time worker, and was taken during a visit to Sunderland in 1918.*

cise its prerogative so as to get rid of the deadlock and secure the passing of the Bill.

"In such circumstances Ministers cannot entertain any doubt that the Sovereign would feel it to be his Constitutional duty to accept their advice.

"The King was pleased," added Lord Oxford, "to signify to me that he accepted the advice of his Ministers."

The King gave no outward sign as to what his personal views were on this subject. But he never thought of a refusal which would have involved the Crown in a struggle with Ministers and their exasperated followers, and happily, sufficient Unionist Peers saved the Crown the painful necessity of creating huge batches of Peers—as Mr. Asquith was prepared to do—by voting with the Government to defeat the Die-hard amendment.

The King came out of the struggle with his reputation as a Constitutional Sovereign firmly established, but with the theoretical problem as to the Crown's freedom to withhold the use of the Prerogative at the Sovereign's pleasure and against the will of Ministers virtually settled against such liberty.

Brief mention must be made of an incident which occurred during the anxious times which followed King George's accession. He was the victim of that particularly odious form of calumny from which none in high position is exempt.

A disgraceful libel had been published in a newspaper called the *Liberator*, printed in Paris, but circulated to some extent in this country. It alleged that the King had contracted a marriage in Malta in 1890 with a daughter of Admiral Sir Michael Culme-Seymour.

A man named Mylius, who had circulated the paper in England, was charged on the information of the Attorney-General with criminal libel. He was tried before the Lord Chief Justice and a special jury in February 1911. It was proved in the clearest manner that the allegation made against His Majesty was an invention from beginning to end, and the defendant, who offered no evidence, was found guilty and sentenced to twelve months' imprisonment.

The sympathy with the King which this vile attack on his personal honour evoked from all classes of his subjects was demonstrated in the following month, when His Majesty, accompanied by the Queen, drove from Buckingham Palace to the Crystal Palace to open the Festival of Empire. The long route was lined throughout by spectators, and Their Majesties were cheered almost continuously and with great enthusiasm both on going and returning from Sydenham.

IV

However, the growing bitterness in politics were soon forgotten in the preparations for the Coronation of King George. The whole of the nation prepared to celebrate this occasion in a fine, patriotic spirit.

The curtain on this Royal cavalcade rose in May, when the preliminary spectacle of the unveiling of the Queen Victoria Memorial opposite Buckingham Palace and the opening of the new Mall and the Admiralty Arch was witnessed by thousands of people.

The personages at this great ceremony little dreamed of how Fate would

THE WAR IS WON. *Huge crowds gathered outside Buckingham Palace on November 11, 1918, when the news of the Armistice was received. King George can be seen on the balcony acknowledging the cheers of the people.*

play with them like wilful puppets. It was to be the last occasion on which the German Emperor was to show himself to a London crowd. Wearing a British field-marshal's uniform, the Kaiser had a definite military bearing. With the Emperor of Germany came the Empress and their only daughter.

Just a year previously, in May 1910, the Kaiser had come to England for the funeral of King Edward VII, to lay a wreath on the coffin of the man whom he had declared to be " A Satan —you cannot imagine what a Satan. . . ." He had also, with the other crowned heads and envoys extraordinary, sat at the State dinner given at Buckingham Palace on that occasion.

Ex-President Roosevelt was also at that dinner, and he has described how he listened to the tearful plaints and cares of the King of Greece. He was then buttonholed by the Tsar of Bulgaria, but the Kaiser promptly contrived to tear the American away from this confabulation, whispering to Roosevelt that Ferdinand was quite unworthy to know him. " In your place I should not speak to him. He is a miserable creature. . . ."

On this second occasion, at the unveiling of the Queen Victoria Memorial, the Kaiser found himself once again at a dinner-party and State ball, given at Buckingham Palace. Again and again the Kaiser sought to ingratiate himself with Lord Kitchener, but in vain. Maybe it was a case of iron men meeting. Kitchener, as usual, had nothing to say.

The unveiling itself took place on May 16. As Sir George Arthur has pointed out, this gigantic piece of statuary has met with no fewer critics than champions, and there have been many to suggest that Queen Victoria was appropriately represented as turning her back on the Palace, which, through fifty years, she was always so reluctant to enter and so eager to leave.

The King and Queen with their Imperial visitors and the Kaiser, walked from the Palace to the foot of the memorial to take part in a brief dedicatory service conducted by the Archbishop of Canterbury, of which the music was finely rendered by the choirs of the Royal Chapels of Westminster Abbey and St. Paul's Cathedral.

The Kaiser deposited a gigantic wreath before the memorial ; the sculptor, Mr. Brock, was presented to the King, who called him back, asked for a sword, and knighted him.

In his reply to an address read by the Chairman of the Memorial Committee, the King paid a finely worded tribute to the greatness of England's greatest Queen, and then passed on to lay emphasis on the presence of the Kaiser and on the " strong and living ties of kinship and friendship " between the thrones and persons of the two sovereigns ; it was hoped that the visit —with the cordial reception which had admittedly delighted the Kaiser—would initiate a definite improvement in Anglo-German relations.

The Kaiser himself must have realised that these hopes were premature. He had not failed to observe that England was in the throes of a big naval campaign, and that the naval estimates for that year had already been increased by nearly £4,000,000. And the North Sea was definitely regarded as the scene of a future conflict between the two great Sea Powers.

Within a year the ties of kinship were to wither into dust, and the ties of friendship were to be irreparably

A REMARKABLE SCENE *when ex-servicemen dashed forward, at the end of a ceremony, to shake their sovereign's hand.*

KING GEORGE *with his son at the Trooping of the Colour in 1919, which was held in Hyde Park.*

PEACE PROCLAMATION. *The heralds performing the ancient ceremony of proclaiming that Britain is again at peace, and the terms under which the war was won.*

broken. And the next occasion when a visit of the Kaiser to England was suggested, was to be made by Mr. Lloyd George, at the election after the Armistice. Then it was boldly proposed that the man responsible for the War and all its miseries should be brought to England as a prisoner and tried for his life by some great tribunal.

As the Kaiser left London for the last time he little realised that some years hence the hoardings would be pasted with slogans : " Hang the Kaiser ! "

And now the actual day of the Coronation approached. London was invaded by vast crowds of people, and it was estimated that altogether some 3,000,000 visitors came to the great city.

Vast wooden stands were fixed up along the route of the procession and troops were brought into the city to line the streets.

On the eve of the great day, June 22, there appeared a huge list of Coronation honours, containing upwards of 550 names, peerages, baronetcies, knighthoods, and privy councillorships, although this was a period when the struggle between the House of Lords and the House of Commons had reached a climax.

The great ceremony itself was held at Westminster Abbey. The Duke of Norfolk, as hereditary Earl Marshal, stage-managed the show. It was estimated that a congregation of some 8,000 people was waiting in the Abbey when the King's procession entered.

Immediately before the Queen, whose train was borne by four duchesses, there was the Archbishop of York and the Archbishop of Canterbury.

The King himself, in his crimson Robes of State and with his train upheld by pages of honour, was followed by the great military and naval officers and personages of his household. The rear was brought up by the Yeomen of the Guard.

The great doors of the Abbey were then closed. Their Majesties went to the Chairs of State near the High Altar and the King then came forward in full view of the congregation to be presented to the Archbishop of Canterbury.

For the first time since 1689, the Coronation Oath was shorn of a paragraph which had given a certain amount of offence to the Roman Catholics of Britain.

Under this amended Coronation Oath, King George was enabled to signify his adherence to the Protestant religion and pledge himself to secure the Protestant succession in the simple terms : " I do solemnly and sincerely in the presence of God profess, testify and declare that I am a faithful member of the Protestant Reformed Church by law established in England, and I will, according to the true intent of the enactment which secures the Protestant succession to the Throne of my Realm, uphold and maintain the said enactment to the best of my power according to Law."

The change must have given special gratification to the Duke of Norfolk, who, as hereditary Earl Marshal, was in charge of the Coronation ceremony —a huge task which went through without a hitch of any kind. The Duke was the leader of the Roman Catholic laity in England, and was held in the highest esteem by all classes and creeds of the King's subjects.

Following upon this, divested of his Robes of State, the King sat on the chair containing the Coronation Stone,

KING GEORGE AND QUEEN MARY *leaving St. Paul's Cathedral after the Thanksgiving Service at the end of the War.*

KING GEORGE TAKING THE SALUTE *from the Royal Pavilion at the Queen Victoria Memorial during the Peace March.*

KING GEORGE AND QUEEN MARY *visiting an L.C.C. school at Pentonville.*

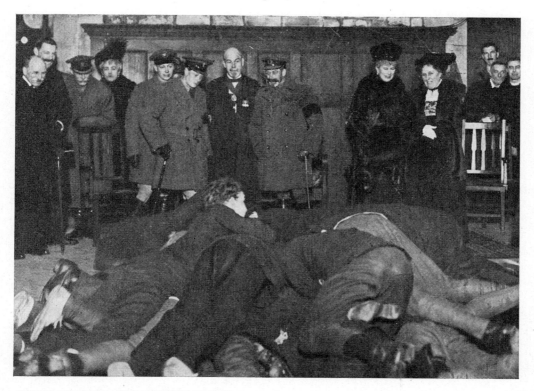

KING GEORGE AND QUEEN MARY *seem to have been highly amused whilst watching the tossing the pancake ceremony at Westminster School.*

with a pall held over his head by four peers who were alike highly placed and familiar friends, while the Primate solemnly anointed his head, breast, and hands.

Then the Royal Robes having been assumed, the Archbishop presented the Orb, with the admonition, " When you see the Orb set under the Cross remember that the whole world is subject to the power and empire of Christ our Redeemer."

The ring and the two sceptres were then handed to the King.

Finally, after Queen Mary had been anointed and crowned and had made her obeisance as the first subject of the Empire to the King Emperor, Westminster Abbey was hushed from east to west and the Holy Sacrament was administered to a kneeling King and Queen in all their gorgeous array.

Not until two o'clock in the afternoon did the King and Queen leave the Abbey to drive along the very circuitous route and receive the plaudits of the great crowds that gathered.

Some 60,000 troops were lining the streets, and all these men and the arrangements had been in the hands of the General Officer Commanding for the occasion, Lord Kitchener. Despite the gigantic scale of these celebrations, it is recorded that there was not a single incident or casualty throughout the whole period.

The third day of the Coronation was celebrated by a review at Spithead of the most formidable fleet that has ever been assembled.

It consisted of no fewer than 165 warships formed in even columns, each nearly five miles in length. There were also present some eighteen foreign warships.

The King and Queen with Princess Mary, the Prince of Wales, and the Duke of York, together with the many Royal guests, travelled by special train to Portsmouth, then embarked in the Royal Yacht *Victoria and Albert*, which steamed along the line.

That night all the ships were illuminated, searchlights scattered the sky, and the Solent was a blaze of light.

Other celebrations included a special State performance at His Majesty's Theatre, and garden parties at Buckingham Palace. Almost every Empire and foreign figure of note was present at these occasions, and London had never seen such a galaxy of figures before.

The illuminations in London made it the brightest city in Europe. Huge crowds drifted about the streets, and observers noted that here was a city at the zenith of its success. Perhaps never again was London to appear so prosperous and happy.

It was during these celebrations that the Prince of Wales came into the public eye. Naturally shy and diffident, and still being fairly young, he had up to this moment kept rather in the background.

Now he mentally shouldered the burdens of ceremonial and State duties which devolved upon him. His dignified appearance in Westminster Abbey during the Coronation of his father was remarked by all. On that occasion the Prince wore his picturesque garter robes and hat. His train was carried by Lord Ashley and his crown borne by Lord Revelstoke.

Immediately after the King was crowned by the Archbishop of Canterbury, the Prince was the first to do homage to the Sovereign. Taking off his crown and kneeling before His Majesty, the Prince said : " I, Prince of

THE CENOTAPH, *erected in Whitehall to the memory of the Glorious Dead, was unveiled by King George on Armistice Day, 1920. It was designed by Sir Edwin Lutyens.*

Wales, do become your liege man of life and limb and of earthly worship ; and faith and truth I will bear unto you, to live and die, against all manner of folks. So help me God."

Having thus rendered homage, the young Prince touched the crown so newly placed on the King's head and kissed the King on his left cheek. The King with outstretched arms drew the Prince towards him and kissed him on the right cheek.

But soon after the Coronation ordeal an even greater welcome awaited the Prince of Wales. This was the Investiture at the historic castle of Carnarvon in Wales.

This was the scene where, many years ago, the infant Edward of Carnarvon was traditionally believed to have been accepted by the people of Wales as their first English Prince.

This was indeed a remarkable celebration, made particularly brilliant by the manner in which the Welsh people set themselves out to make the affair one of great patriotism and national enthusiasm.

On a splendid sunshine day in June the little town of Carnarvon was packed with loyal Welshmen and people from every part of the King's dominion.

The Prince of Wales, wearing his midshipman's uniform, arrived by train and drove to the castle, where his first duty was to receive an address from the Corporation of the borough of Carnarvon.

The Prince's reply—the first speech in which a Prince of Wales had used the Welsh language—is worth quoting :

" I thank you most sincerely for your kind welcome and address. It gives me great pleasure to visit your historic town. I have read how, as Segontium, it was famous in the days of the Romans, and your noble castle has especial interest for me. I have already heard some of your far-famed singing, of which I have been told so much. It gives me great delight. It touches all who hear it, coming as it does from the heart as well as from the head. As we say, ' Mor o gan yw Cymru i gyd " (' All Wales is a sea of song ').

" When I think of the many links which bind me to our beautiful country, the title I bear seems more real to me than ever. You greet me on behalf of all in your ancient mother tongue with 'Croesaw' ('Welcome'), and let me end by saying ' Diolch o waelod fy nghalon i hen wlad fy nhadau ' (' Thanks from the bottom of my heart to the old land of my fathers ')."

The King had also to receive an address from the Corporation, and in his reply used words which will long be remembered in Wales. His Majesty said :

" I believe that the occasion will serve a still deeper purpose in assembling in union and power around the Prince's person all the forces of Welsh national life which preserve the fame and achievements of your historic ancestors, and will sustain in the world of modern times the virtues of the British race and the glories of the British Empire."

The procession which conducted the Prince to the Chamberlain's Tower, where he was robed for the ceremony, recalled the ancient pageantry of a people who have preserved their national customs and national privileges in a manner which is beyond all praise.

Heralds, the Archdruid and Druids matched the surroundings of the medieval castle, whilst the martial glories of Wales were recalled by the presence of

KING GEORGE *placing a wreath upon the coffin of the Unknown Soldier, November 11, 1920.*

the Welch Regiment and other national military formations.

The King and Queen wore none of the panoplies of their exalted rank on this occasion.

The King was merely an Admiral of the great Service to which his son belonged, and the Queen was only a beautiful and gracious lady proudly attending a ceremony in which her firstborn was playing the leading part.

The Prince's sister added to the family character of the ceremony. She wore a pretty white frock and hat, and her girlish simplicity and charming appearance won all hearts.

Mr. Lloyd George, as Constable of the Castle, received Their Majesties, and handed the King the great key of the Castle, which His Majesty received and handed back to his Constable.

The King and Queen seated themselves on two thrones, with a vacant throne on the King's right hand, and His Majesty then summoned the Prince to the Presence through the Earl Marshal.

The Prince soon appeared, preceded by heralds and pursuivants and great nobles bearing his Insignia.

He was followed by the officers of his household. His youth was marked by the presence of his tutor amongst these gallant gentlemen.

The Prince wore a picturesque kit consisting of a short purple surcoat, white knee-breeches, and white stockings. He had no head-dress, as hats belong to a later period than his medieval uniform. He kneeled at the King's feet whilst the Home Secretary read the Letters Patent of his appointment, and then did homage in the ancient formula which he had already repeated at the King's Coronation.

Rising, he was kissed by the King and placed on the vacant throne by the King's side.

An eloquent address was then delivered by Sir John Rhys, to which the Prince replied :

" I thank you with all my heart for your cordial welcome, and with you I wish that this may be the first of many visits to our beautiful country. As your address reminds me, the many links of the past, my Tudor descent, the great title that I bear, as well as my name David, all bind me to Wales, and to-day I can safely say that I am in ' hen wlad fy nhadau ' (' the old land of my fathers ').

" I assure you that I shall never forget to-day as long as I live, and I hope sincerely that it will always mark a happy day in the Principality as one which brought you a new friend. He is, it is true, a young friend—I am very young—but I have great examples before me. I have my dear father and my dear mother and good friends to help me, and so, bearing in mind our ancient and beautiful saying, ' Heb Dduw, heb ddim ; Duw a digon ' (' Without God, without anything ; God is enough ') I hope to do my duty to my King, to Wales, and to you all."

The use of the Welsh language by the young Prince a second time aroused immense enthusiasm, and after a short religious service conducted by not only the bishops of the Welsh dioceses, but representatives of the Free Churches of Wales, the King presented their Prince to his people.

Four times the Prince appeared to the waiting throngs outside the castle and four times he was greeted with a musical welcome which only Welsh people could give.

THE ROYAL BRIDE *is pelted with confetti by her three brothers in the Buckingham Palace courtyard. A scene at the wedding of Princess Mary to Viscount Lascelles, now Earl of Harewood.*

KING GEORGE WITH KING ALBERT *of the Belgians during the latter's visit to London in* 1921.

KING GEORGE AND QUEEN MARY *with the King and Queen of the Belgians.*

KING GEORGE *always enjoyed horse-riding, and until the later years of his life was out regularly every morning. Here he is seen in Windsor Park with his sons.*

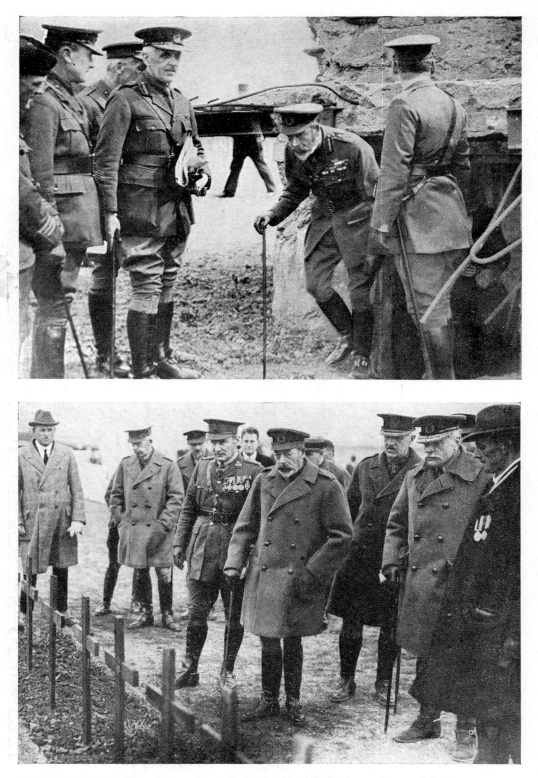

AFTER THE WAR *King George visited the battlefields. In the lower photograph he is seen inspecting a German cemetery.*

KING GEORGE AND QUEEN MARY *visited the Chelsea Flower Show regularly. They showed a keen interest in the exhibits, many of which were from the Royal nurseries at Windsor.*

When at last the Sovereign led the Prince to the King's Gate for the last presentation, the final welcome must have touched the heart of the most hardened cynic.

The singing of the " Land of my Fathers " and of the " Old Hundredth " by the assembled multitude produced a volume of stirring melody which could not have been achieved anywhere except in the land which the Prince had claimed as a " Sea of Song."

It was a wonderful and unforgettable pageant, but must have been a trying experience for a youth of seventeen.

Yet no sooner had these national celebrations ended than the clouds began to gather over Europe. Various startling incidents revealed that the world was rapidly drifting towards that war which already men were talking about, thinking about, and fearing in their own hearts.

As usual, it was an incident in an out-of-the-way part of the world which provoked the Powers into threatening each other. It was in Morocco, where France was rapidly extending her empire and had almost completely taken possession of that country.

Germany, feeling that she had been left out of that African Empire, this great scramble for a continent which had been going on for some years, ordered the German gunboat *Panther* to sail to the port of Agadir in Morocco.

It was really a definite gesture against France, and, in order that France might continue her occupation of Morocco, Germany in return demanded the whole of the Congo as the price of her goodwill, or non-interference. Britain, although apparently not concerned in this dispute, did not hesitate to warn Germany of the consequences of her action.

Mr. Lloyd George, who might be said to have been the least imperialistic of all the Cabinet Ministers in Britain, made a startling speech at the Mansion House, which conveyed a note of warning to Germany. He even spoke of " Teutonic bullying."

Three days later there were rumours of orders for the British Fleet to stand by, although Mr. Asquith, then Prime Minister, promptly made a statement that there was no question of intervention at Agadir by Britain.

Although this affair began to blow over, it was obvious to acute observers that the World Powers were jostling each other for position. The war seemed inevitable. Only Germany realised that the time was not quite ripe.

At the same time many of the European nations were scrambling for the loot which followed on the break-up of the Turkish Empire. Italy seized Tripoli and the twelve Ægean Islands off the Asia Minor coast. Germany, never noted for shrewd diplomacy, stood by baffled while this loot was being seized.

V

Throughout the Coronation festivities King George conceived an idea which in its bearing and originality was to be of the utmost importance to India, the great empire of which he had been crowned Emperor.

He had decided that the Oriental splendours of the great city of Delhi, once the seat of the Mogul emperors, should be restored again. Since the British occupation of India, Calcutta

A FAMILY GROUP, *taken after the wedding of the Duke and Duchess of York.*

had been the seat of Government. Now King George was to revive the importance of long-neglected Delhi.

In November the King and Queen sailed for India. Already as Prince of Wales he had visited India in 1905 and revealed himself as a great sportsman, and a big-game hunter of no mean ability.

But he had not neglected to study the Indian political situation, as was shown in his own words at the conclusion of that early visit :

" I cannot help thinking, the more I have heard and seen, that the task of governing India will be mainly easier if we, on our part, infuse into it a wider element of sympathy.   I will venture to predict that to such sympathy there will be an ever abundant and genuine response."

In this State visit to India, for the magnificent Durbar to be held at Delhi, the King Emperor was to reveal that those early words of his had a meaning.

The Royal voyage to India was made in the *Medina*, a new ship of the P. and O. line, a great company which has maintained regular connection between England and the East for half a century.

For the time being the *Medina* became a King's ship, and a third mast was stepped to enable His Majesty to fly all three flags, which indicate the presence of the Sovereign—the Royal Standard at the main, the Admiralty flag at the fore, and the Union Jack at the mizzen.

A tremendous reception was held when the King and Queen arrived, but very soon they were proceeding up country for the great Durbar to be held at Delhi.

Months of work had created a great imperial camp in Delhi. Splendid new roads, lighted with powerful lamps, were constructed, a polo ground was created, and gardens resplendent with flowers sprang into being. Few people could realise that a short year before, the site had been brown desert land.

The days and nights preceding the Durbar were crowded with events. There were receptions of ruling chiefs. India believes in pageantry, as also in the mysteriousness and aloofness of its emperors.

King George, as Emperor of India, decided that his arrival in Delhi should be impressive as well as spectacular. He arranged to enter the great fortress of Delhi and come forth and show himself to the multitude as had the Mogul emperors in other days.

The day when the King rode forth from the Delhi gates to the great camp and amphitheatre that had been prepared in his honour was, indeed, a memorable occasion to the Indian people.

The road itself was one along which the old Mogul emperors had passed in ceremonial procession with palanquins, elephants, and glittering trappings of all kinds. Tens of thousands of Indians comprising the various peoples of this great empire were lining the routes. They had been crowding into the city for weeks beforehand. Many of them had slept and eaten and lived along the line of the route.

One holy man was said to have trekked four months without ceasing in order to be present on this great occasion. After having seen the Emperor pass he started on his return journey, happy in having beheld " The Shadow of God on Earth."

The windows of the crazy Oriental houses were crowded with spectators, veiled women peeped from lattice

KING GEORGE AND QUEEN MARY, *with Queen Alexandra and the Princes, at the wedding of Princess Maud.*

windows, coloured turbans of every description were seen.

Thousands of troops paraded the two-miles route. British and Indian cavalry trotted to and fro, the pennants of their lances fluttering in the slight breeze.

Besides the British Army in full ceremonial uniform, there was also the whole pageantry of Indian military display. It included Baluchis in cherry and green uniforms, Sikhs and Pathans in khaki. There was the North-west Frontier Regiment in blue and grey. Several Gurkha regiments were parading, and also the Camel Corps riding on their huge brown beasts. Altogether some 50,000 troops took part in this procession from the gates of Delhi.

The King Emperor himself had an escort of the leading princes of India. These princes wore glistening coats of mail and steel armour which caught the bright sunshine and glittered against the eyes of the watching multitudes.

The Governors of the various provinces of India led the procession. Then came Lord Kitchener in full uniform, a striking figure as Commander-in-Chief to the Emperor.

He was followed by a glittering group of Imperial Heralds, with trumpets. Then came the senior corps of the Indian Army, the Governor-General's bodyguard raised in 1777 by Warren Hastings, a superbly mounted contingent drawn from the pick of the fighting races of India.

It was separated from the Emperor by an escort of His Majesty's Life Guards and Royal Horse Guards, which had fittingly accompanied the Sovereign. Their glittering breastplates and plumed helmets gave them a special appeal, even in that dazzling array of gorgeous uniforms.

Finally came the King Emperor himself, in the dress of a field-marshal and bestriding a magnificent dark brown Australian charger.

The one disappointment of the big, eager-eyed multitude was that the King Emperor was wearing a plumed helmet, which, to some extent, shaded his familiar features from the crowd.

Many of the natives also expected the Emperor to be riding in a howdah on top of a huge elephant. The fact that he was astride a horse and wearing a uniform which seemed to them rather like that of any British general was to some extent a disappointment. Many of the natives missed him altogether. Seeing the Queen alone in a carriage, regal in bearing and marked out by the gorgeous fan and umbrella, the multitude murmured that the King was not in the procession at all.

However, the Durbar left no doubt in their minds. Here was a King Emperor indeed, seated on a throne and wearing the Royal crown.

The Durbar was held on December 12 in the large amphitheatre which had been specially prepared. Some 10,000 spectators, including all the great officials of India, filled the semi-circular stand. In the very centre of this huge semi-circle was the Royal dais under a gorgeous canopy.

Their Majesties wore their crowns and Coronation robes and sat on special thrones, while the heralds read the Royal proclamation in English and Urdu, ending with a fanfare of trumpets and rolling of drums.

The arena itself was occupied by 20,000 troops of all arms, and, outside the amphitheatre, a mound had been built up to accommodate 50,000 natives.

Standing stiffly to attention at one

KING GEORGE *took a loyal interest in his subjects' amusements. He frequently visited the Cup Final, and is here seen shaking hands with the Manchester City team which played at Wembley in* 1926.

KING GEORGE AND QUEEN MARY *in the cab of the Royal special engine, during a visit to the G.W.R. shops at Swindon in* 1924.

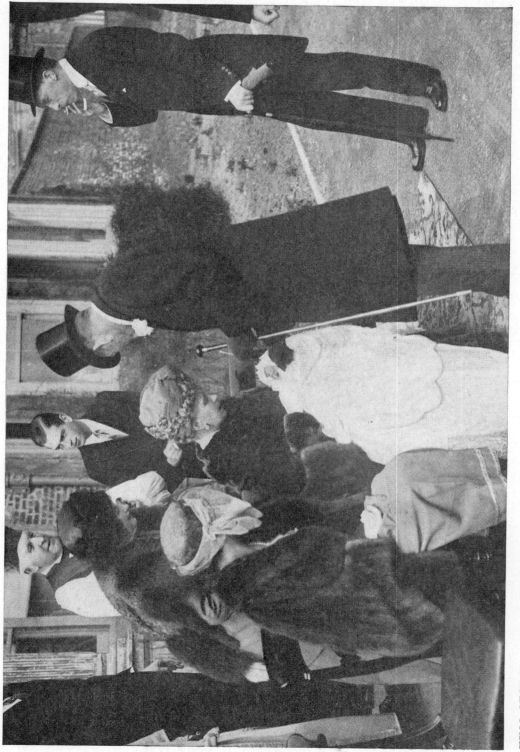

KING GEORGE AND QUEEN MARY *with Viscount Lascelles, their first grandson and son of Princess Royal and the Earl of Harewood.*

KING GEORGE AND QUEEN MARY *rarely visited a cinema, and films were usually shown to them privately. This photograph was taken during a visit to the Marble Arch Pavilion, to see a naval film, where they were received by Earl Beatty.*

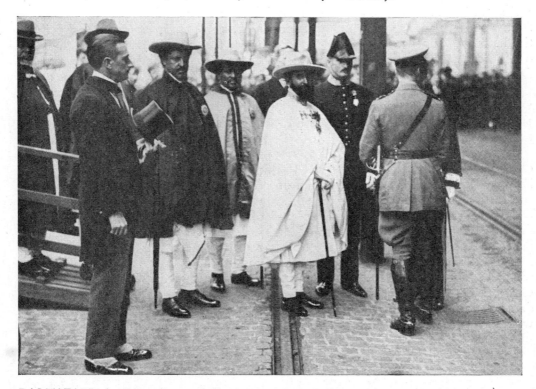

RAS TAFARI, *then Prince Regent of Abyssinia, visited England in 1924. He was entertained by King George upon several occasions.*

corner of the pavilion beneath which sat Their Majesties was a solitary and striking figure. It was a British Grenadier, wearing the bearskin familiar in Europe, but never seen in India before. Despite the sunshine, this superb figure never flinched, and at the end of his long period of duty was found to be none the worse.

The Emperor and his Consort then received the homage of India. Procession after procession passed. Thunder after thunder of artillery roared its salute.

Finally, when the last salute had been sounded and the Viceroy by the King Emperor's order had read a proclamation of boons to be conferred in honour of the day, the chief herald stood up to his full height in his stirrups and, doffing his helmet, called for three cheers for the King Emperor, and three more for the Queen Empress.

A final fanfare from the trumpeters, and then, in a clear voice, the King read from a slip of paper news which startled the listening crowds.

The capital of India was to be transferred from Calcutta to Delhi.

The announcement was received with tremendous enthusiasm, cheering, shouting, weeping, by the many multitudes of India present.

Later, Their Majesties moved to another pavilion, where they received the homage first of the Viceroy and then of the Indian princes.

It was a scene of unforgettable splendour. The princes wore magnificent robes and priceless jewels, and the ceremony of doing homage to their Emperor was an education in Indian customs. One prince, carrying a cane and finely dressed, would only bow, whilst another would lay his sword or white scarf at the feet of Their Majesties. This caused some misunderstanding in one place, and an Indian prince had to explain away an act of apparent discourtesy.

But that this great Durbar had aroused India to a fever of imperial patriotism was revealed by an incident which occurred at the end. It is described by Col. R. J. Blackman.

The thousands of people who had been watching from the mound outside suddenly surged across the vacant arena like a huge oncoming wave, which swelled up to the steps of the pavilion, the place where the Sovereign had been sitting.

This sudden and unexpected flood of people at first caused some alarm to the military guard of Highlanders which was stationed round the vacant throne.

The people were impelled by an irresistible impulse to approach the sacred places where the Emperor had been. They swarmed up the pavilion on every side, and men of all races and religions prostrated themselves before the empty throne, or strained over one another's heads to touch with just the tips of their fingers the fringe of the carpet on which Their Majesties had stood.

This extraordinary scene, which will remain deeply rooted in the memory of those who witnessed it, was most impressively touching, a striking manifestation of the great spiritual idea underlying the respect and affection of Eastern people for their Sovereign.

Eventually, with some difficulty, a regular queue was formed, the people passing up one side and down the other. It was estimated that over 200,000 persons thus passed before the throne, to say nothing of the many more who followed on the succeeding days.

A PERSISTENT GIPSY BEGGAR *chasing King George's carriage whilst on his way to a race meeting.*

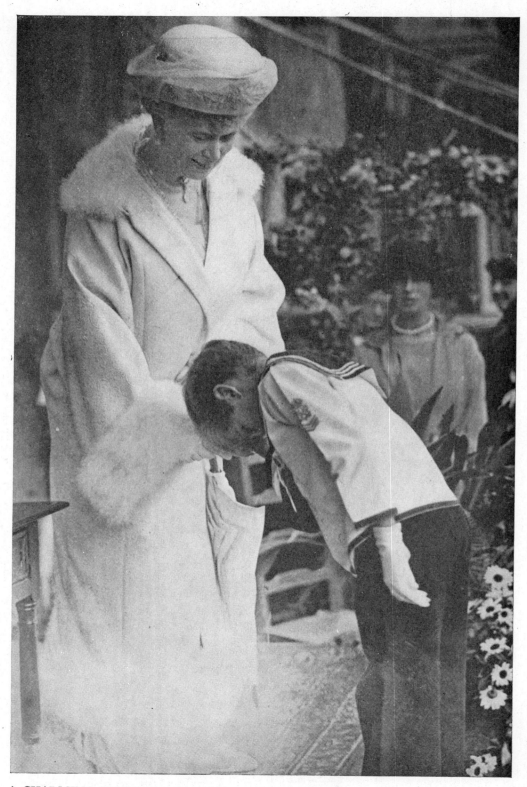

A CHARMING PICTURE *of Queen Mary receiving a £500 cheque for charity from Lady Astor's youngest son.*

The following day saw a great national festival, filled with all the displays and shows in which the Indian revels. It was the people's day, with musical rides, daring displays of horsemanship, groups of jugglers, and other variety entertainment.

Suddenly on a balcony of the old fortress overlooking this joyous scene appeared the King and Queen, unheralded by any trumpets. In an instant they were seen and recognised by the great crowd. There was an upward surge of dark arms in salute and a great shout of acclaim rent the air.

From the balcony Their Majesties passed to two thrones on the ramparts in order to come more entirely within view. And for hours the people filed past them, unrestrained by police or military, until with the sunset King George and his Queen returned to camp.

Then came the great review of the troops who had been gathered together in Delhi for these celebrations. To the number of 40,000 they paraded, British and Indian, horse, foot, and guns, going through the many complicated movements of a pre-war review.

Then came the charge of cavalry, frenzied dashing, clattering masses of clans, each trying to beat the other in the speed with which they galloped across the plains.

One of the great moments was when the boy Maharajah of Bahawalpur, a tiny figure on a great war camel, leading his own regiment of bearded warriors, passed the King Emperor, his baby arm touching the toy sword outstretched in perfect salute.

The final scene of that glittering Durbar was the investiture held by the King Emperor in the gardens of Delhi Park, which had once seen the magnificence of the Moguls.

Many orders and decorations were bestowed. The first to enter was the Queen Empress, who, dressed in pale blue, a colour which for so many years she has specially affected, knelt before the King to receive the Star of India.

It was a touching scene when Her Majesty kissed the hand of her Sovereign.

After these many ceremonies the King left Delhi and journeyed to Nepal to enjoy ten days' big-game shooting. Many fine tigers were bagged on this great hunt.

This visit of the King Emperor and Queen Empress to India has never been forgotten. It is still remembered as the glittering pageant by the multitudes of India. It has done more perhaps, during the persistent attempts of unrest engineered by agitators in the East, to hold the patriotism of the people and retain their unswerving loyalty.

The time was swiftly coming when the King Emperor was to call upon the millions in India to join in the World War, which was even then rumbling on the great horizon.

At noon on January 8 the King and Queen left Calcutta for Bombay under a final salute of 101 guns from the ramparts of Fort William. Tears streamed down the face of the Maharajah Scindia of Gwalior, and Sir Pertab Singh, toughened warrior though he was, could only stammer that he was growing an old man, for he, too, broke down under stress of emotion.

On the 10th the shores of India faded in the *Medina's* wake as the King left the empire which had spread itself at his feet.

VI

Events, unknown to the vast multitudes who would soon be at grips in a life and death struggle, were hurrying on apace. The various foreign Chancelleries were in a highly nervous state. Foreign affairs seemed to be sliding into chaos. Treaties and counter-treaties and secret understandings were already ranging the future protagonists.

But in Britain the dangerous state of Europe was ignored because of the dangerous state of affairs at home. King George was engaged day and night in unwearying and tactful efforts to prevent a real disaster to the Constitution. And in the midst of all these State worries there were the public ceremonies to be undertaken.

In 1913 the King was present in person at the memorial service at St. Paul's Cathedral to pay last honours to Captain Scott, Captain Oates, and their companions, lost on their return from the South Pole, and then the Court was thrown into mourning by the news of the assassination of the King of the Hellenes, on March 17.

Reviews of troops in London and at Aldershot and an inspection of the Royal Military College at Sandhurst, preceded the departure of the King and Queen to Germany, where it was hoped that a long-standing feud caused by the claims of the Duke of Cumberland to the Hanoverian throne would be settled by the marriage of the German Emperor's only daughter to Prince Ernest of Cumberland, to whom the Kaiser presented as a wedding gift the Grand Duchy of Brunswick. King George is reported to have expressed his doubt whether any final reconciliation was likely to be thus achieved, and events proved that his opinion was correct.

During a tour in Lancashire, in the opening months of 1914, the King was recalled to London by the famous Curragh episode. It was essentially a matter dealing with party politics, and as such properly outside the intervention of the Crown. But as the incident had taken place among members of His Majesty's Army, and it was asserted that the unwillingness of the officers to lead their men against Ulstermen had been combated by the official statement that it was the personal order of the Sovereign that they should do so, the King was deeply interested in the strange incident.

The assertion was totally untrue, but the intimate relations that existed between the King and his Army made it necessary that he should be in London while such grave political events were in progress as the resignation of the Secretary of State for War, the assumption of his office by the Prime Minister, and the retirement of Sir John French (afterwards Lord Ypres), Chief of the Imperial Staff, and of the Adjutant-General, Sir John Ewart. By April 21 the crisis was over, and Their Majesties were able to carry out a long-promised return visit of three days to the President of the French Republic.

There was a Midland tour in June, and a Scottish tour early in July. A full mobilisation of the Fleet at Spithead next demanded His Majesty's presence.

So far did the horizon seem that the King's inability to keep his engagement to be there on July 17 was due, not to any shadow forecast by the international situation, but to the ever-growing seriousness of the refusal of North-East Ulster to accept Home Rule in any circumstances or conditions.

THE BRITISH EMPIRE EXHIBITION at Wembley was the great event of 1924 and 1925. It was opened in State by King George on April 23, 1924, and was attended by almost the entire Royal Family and members of the Cabinet.

KING GEORGE *at the tomb of France's Unknown Soldier during a visit to Paris in* 1925.

KING GEORGE *went for a cruise in the Mediterranean in* 1925 *to recover from an illness. He visited Palermo amongst other places.*

QUEEN ALEXANDRA *with her great-grandson, Viscount Lascelles. The photograph was
taken a few months before her death.*

THE ENTIRE COUNTRY *mourned the death of Queen Alexandra, widow of Edward VII, in November 1925 ; and, despite a snowstorm, huge crowds gathered at her funeral to pay a last tribute. She was buried at Windsor.*

The King thereupon personally intervened in the Irish question with the fullest approval of his Ministers. He invited representatives of both sides to meet at a round-table conference in Buckingham Palace. The first meeting was on July 21. On the 24th the hopelessness of coming to any agreement was manifest; the last device of a harassed Government had failed. In a fortnight it had also been forgotten, swallowed up in the outbreak of the World War.

This was a time of anxious days and nights at Buckingham Palace. Always the King was at work in his study, scrutinising documents, interviewing political personages of all sides, endeavouring to find the formula that would be acceptable to all parties.

And now the shadow of a great international conflict was clouding the whole sky. Foreign Office officials were constantly coming and going at Buckingham Palace. As the situation became more acute, King George intervened personally with telegrams to the Czar, the Kaiser, and other rulers to prevent this hysterical madness that was leading all nations towards a terrible conflict.

They were times when King George rarely left that study in Buckingham Palace. He worked through the long hours of the night into the dawn, striving desperately for the peace which day by day grew more hopeless.

Yet the wisdom and the foresight of King George were to prove themselves in ironic fashion to those crowned heads of Europe who refused to heed his pleas for peace. For all of them, with the exception of King George himself, were to lose their thrones. The Kings who insisted upon war really committed self-suicide; the one King who insisted upon peace retained the loyalty and affection of his people.

One often wonders at the mixed, emotional feelings that must have affected King George on that evening in August 1914 when, in response to the cheering clamour of crowds outside Buckingham Palace, he stepped forth on to the balcony to be greeted by a thunderous shout.

Once again Britain was at war. Many in that cheering crowd would later be dead and maimed things on foreign battlefields or, as Masefield wrote of the dead in the Dardanelles—" dumb things pushed by the tides."

For the moment they were filled with the intoxicating idea of going to war for their King and country, although the King they now loudly acclaimed had striven night and day to save them from such a terrible ordeal. Only those who stood in the shadows behind King George, as he acknowledged the shouting and singing of the crowds, saw that tears were dimming his eyes. The sorrows of a King come oftener than the joys.

KING GEORGE *with the Prime Minister of England and the Dominions Premiers at the*
1926 Imperial Conference in London.

CHATTING WITH A CHILD PATIENT *during a visit to a children's hospital.*

WITH KING BORIS OF BULGARIA *during the latter's visit to England.*

A FAMILY GROUP *at the christening of Princess Elizabeth.*

KING GEORGE AND QUEEN MARY AT BUCKINGHAM PALACE, 1926.

KING GEORGE *in the impressive robes of the Order of the Garter.*

SHAKING HANDS WITH HIS UNCLE, *the Duke of Connaught, when they met at an installation ceremony of the Order of the Bath at Westminster Abbey.*

CHAPTER V

EUROPE AT WAR

Assassination at Sarajevo—Austria's ultimatum to Servia—Alarming messages from Russia—Austria declares war—King George's appeal to the Czar—Russia and Germany at war—Britain's ultimatum—Britain at war.

I

THE drama of Sarajevo has been told again and again. But by its apparent insignificance to the peoples beyond the Balkans it has an ironic fatality which makes its retelling a necessity in the true history of these twenty-five years of King George's reign.

The scene of that shot that began the Great War was Sarajevo, a city in the provinces of Bosnia-Herzegovina, a Balkan country which had been incorporated within the boundaries of Austria-Hungary.

The peoples of those newly acquired territories were thought to be hostile to the rule of the old Emperor Francis Josef, and for that reason it was considered wise to arrange a Royal demonstration and procession in the streets of Sarajevo itself.

The Royal figure chosen for this demonstration of the might of Austria-Hungary was the heir to the throne himself, Franz Ferdinand, Archduke of Austria.

Accompanied by his wife, Sophie Chotek, Duchess of Hohenburg, he decided to make a formal entry into the town of Sarajevo on Sunday, June 28, 1914. Incidentally, that day was also the anniversary of his wedding.

The Archduke and his wife were staying at Ilidzhe, a watering-place a few miles from Sarajevo, from which Franz Ferdinand had just directed the military manœuvres.

In his entry to the town of Sarajevo he was to pass along a wide street, on one side of which was a wall and the River Milyatsa. There were three bridges across the river, one of which he was to cross. Five assassins were waiting for him near the first bridge ; one, a boy, Princip, at the second ; and one more at the third.

A little after ten o'clock on that fateful morning the Royal party arrived from Ilidzhe in four cars. As they drove rather swiftly along the street near the first bridge one of the conspirators threw a bomb. It bounced off the Archduke's car and wounded several spectators as well as a lieutenant-colonel in the Archducal suite.

But the cars drove on to the Hôtel de Ville. There the party were received by the Mayor of Sarajevo, who, not knowing what had happened, began an address of loyal welcome on behalf of the citizens. Franz Ferdinand interrupted him and said there was not much loyalty in bombs. A few minutes later an officer announced that they had arrested the man who threw the bomb.

THE ROYAL GARDEN PARTIES, given at Buckingham Palace, were big social events of the season. King George and Queen Mary moved freely among their guests, chatting to their friends

EACH YEAR DURING ASCOT WEEK *King George and Queen Mary paid regular visits. During their reign, this annual event gained added social importance.*

KING GEORGE AND QUEEN MARY *acknowledging the cheers of crippled children whilst on their way to Ascot.*

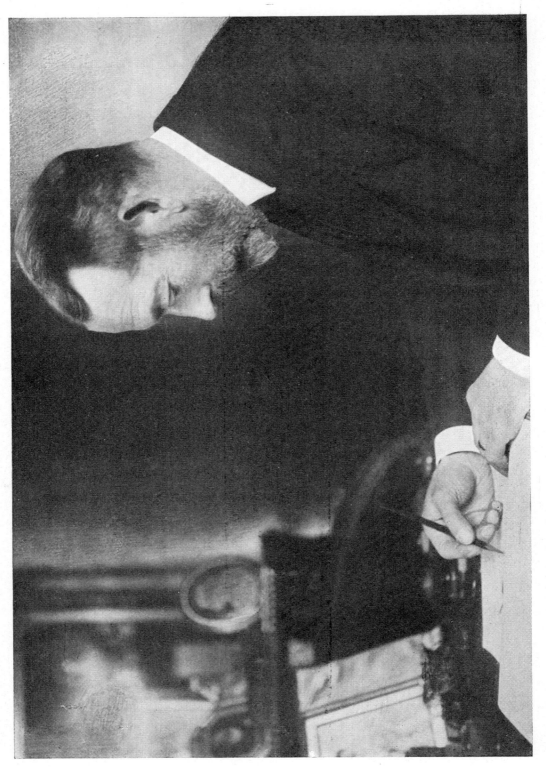

KING GEORGE *in his study at Buckingham Palace.*

" Better hurry and hang him," said the Archduke laconically, " or they will be sending him a decoration from Vienna."

Then the Archduke decided to visit his wounded aide-de-camp at the hospital and the Duchess declared that she would go with him. They set off again —but the driver of the car made a mistake. Instead of driving straight over the bridge he made a turn to the right. Seeing his mistake, he backed the car to turn.

This was the moment for Princip, standing there in the crowd. He jumped forward and fired with his revolver. He hit the Archduke first. He then fired at Potiorek, the military governor, but hit instead the Duchess, who had flung herself forward to protect her husband. They were hurried at once to the Konak, or official residence. The Duchess was dead before they reached there, and Franz Ferdinand died in about ten minutes. It was just eleven o'clock in the morning.

Immediately the telegraph was buzzing with the news across Europe. In Servia itself the news was received with great excitement. In Belgrade, the capital of Servia, the Government, fearing lest in the heat of the excitement aroused by the patriotic rejoicings which were taking place the chauvinist element might lend an anti-Austrian colour to the demonstrations, issued an order to the effect that, as a sign of mourning, all places of entertainment, including cafés, should turn out lights and close at ten o'clock.

Three days later, on July 2, the bodies of the Archduke and his consort reached Vienna. There was no special military display to receive them, though the Archduke was head of the Army.

Next day they lay in state in the Hofburg Chapel.

At four o'clock in the afternoon a funeral service was held at which only a few diplomats were present, and some of the courtiers.

It lasted for a quarter of an hour only, out of regard for the old Emperor. There was no opportunity for the public to pay their respects to the dead.

A great part of the Vienna garrison followed the bodies in the evening to the Western Railway station. At the last moment a large contingent of Vienna notables, who had received no invitations to the funeral, followed the procession on foot as a mark of respect.

At eleven o'clock in the evening the train left for Pochlarn, which it reached about one in the morning of July 14.

A terrible storm burst and the coffins were hurried into the tiny waiting-room of the village station. In the early dawn the hearse was put on a ferry to go over the Danube. Lightning and thunder made the horses shy and they almost precipitated the hearse into the river. The roads at Artstetten were impassable, and the mourners had to wade in the river.

Finally the bodies were borne up the hill to the vault. " The ceremony at the Chapel of Artstetten," says the Archduke's physician, " was simple but dignified." At a sharp turn at the entrance to the vault the bearers knocked the coffin against an edge of the wall, breaking loose a piece. "I saw the picture of the Archduke rise before my eyes, as, upon viewing the vault which was being completed, he jokingly said to me, ' Then I shall turn in my grave.' "

Although the news of this assassination caused the windows of the Foreign Office in Wilhelmstrasse at Berlin and in St. Petersburg to be lighted night after night whilst couriers dashed about with important messages, it seemed that the diplomatic world in general was not unduly perturbed.

The Kaiser himself was on his Royal yacht refreshing himself in the cool Scandinavian fjords.

A few weeks previously, as Admiral of the Fleet, he had been host at Kiel to a squadron of British warships, H.M.S. *King George*, H.M.S. *Ajax*, H.M.S. *Audacious*, and H.M.S. *Centurion*. They were ranged alongside the fine dreadnoughts of Germany's High Fleet.

British and German officers as well as the ordinary seamen and marines had fraternised as good comrades. One of the German commanders noted a toast drunk privately between the German and the British Admirals, " To the White Nations." None of them at that time realised that they would later be meeting in the greatest sea fight of history off Jutland.

At the same time, by the irony of circumstance, the Light Squadron of Admiral Sir Christopher Craddock cruised companionably in Mexican waters with the German ships of Admiral Graf von Spee. At that time Coronel and the Falkland Islands were merely names on the charts carried in the chart-room of each of the ships.

Even in the Wilhelmstrasse the ministers of the German Foreign Office were enjoying their summer holidays. Von Moltke was taking a cure. A certain Colonel Ludendorff, zealous officer of the General Staff, on duty at Strasburg, was taking a few days' leave in the Bavarian hills.

A retired general of blameless and unexciting career, Von Hindenburg, stalked about his Pomeranian country place in gaiters and a shooting jacket.

And even in England, despite the Irish situation, there was little to disturb the serenity of affairs. There was a great naval review off Spithead, King George's ships coming up in columns from the misty sea, to thunder their salutes before the King.

Officers and men of the ships were looking forward to the leave which was to follow this review. Lord Kitchener, who had just been appointed to a command in Egypt, had booked his passage. Only Mr. Winston Churchill, studying plans and charts, and particularly the rather alarming messages coming from diplomats in various European countries, sat in the Admiralty awaiting events.

Even in Paris nobody seemed to realise that the hour had struck, Paris was as gay as ever, and M. Poincaré, as French President, was giving a series of brilliant receptions. Only a month previously King George and Queen Mary had visited Paris, and there had been scenes of enthusiasm and brilliance which revealed that the *entente cordiale* was still on the same firm base that his father, King Edward VII, had placed it.

St. Petersburg, a capital which now no longer exists, was still the scene of romance, mystery, and luxury. Russian princes and grand dukes, with their ladies, were spread about Europe, enjoying themselves in the playgrounds of the rich. Few people paid attention to the fact that in Ekaterinburg, a garrison town just beyond the Urals, a man named Stalin was well guarded in a political prison on the far side of Siberia. At the same time an obscure agitator, Nikolai Lenin, had settled in Switzerland.

And even in Vienna itself there did not seem to be undue excitement over this assassination. The Emperor Franz Josef had known many sorrows in his long life, and he bore this one with more than Christian fortitude. The late Archduke had been a man of liberal tendencies and independent mind, unusual and unbecoming to a Hapsburg. Furthermore, the old Emperor had never approved the marriage with the Countess Chotek.

The next in line was the young Archduke Karl, more amenable and more conscious of the great considerations hedging about the oldest throne in Europe.

Many of these diplomats and others looked back upon a Europe that had been at peace for more than forty years. It did not seem conceivable that war would come now.

The only thing that seemed to be agitating New York was the fact that a very ordinary painting entitled " September Morn " had been suppressed. Some critics had said that the little lady, shivering without a bathing suit in the cold water of sunrise, was lewd and lascivious. Other art critics objected equally as strongly to the ban. Subsequently the ban was removed, and, as was only to be expected, copies of the painting were sold everywhere.

Nevertheless, the assassination of an Archduke could not be ignored by Austria-Hungary. An official investigation had been ordered by the Austro-Hungarian Government into the circumstances leading to the murder of the Archduke.

As a result of this enquiry it was revealed that, although there were indications that the plot to assassinate the Archduke had been concocted in Servia itself, there was nothing to prove or even lead one to suspect the complicity of the Servian Government in the suggestion or preparation of the crime or the providing of the weapons.

Before drawing up their ultimatum to Servia, however, the Emperor Franz Josef and his advisers made diplomatic enquiries in Germany as to whether that country and the Kaiser would support them in the event of war with Russia.

Apparently the Kaiser gave every assurance that Germany would stand by Austria-Hungary.

On July 21, therefore, Austria presented an ultimatum to Servia. Two days later, on a Saturday, the Prime Minister of Servia brought the Servian reply to the ultimatum to Baron Giesl, the Austro-Hungarian Minister in Belgrade. The Prime Minister of Servia said, " We have accepted part of your demand. For the rest we rely upon your loyalty and chivalry. We have always been quite satisfied with you."

Baron Giesl took up the reply of the Servian Government and studied the note for a few moments. Then he turned and looked at the Prime Minister. " The term fixed in the note," he said, " having expired without a satisfactory reply, I have the honour to inform you that I am leaving Belgrade this evening with the staff of my Legation."

And that evening Baron Giesl left the Embassy en route for Vienna. War was now declared between Austria and Servia.

In the meantime the diplomatic excitement had not passed unnoticed in

Russia. The Crown Prince of Servia, seeking desperately for help, had applied personally to the Czar.

The Czar did not hesitate to reply quickly. " When your Royal Highness applied to me at a time of especial stress," he telegraphed, " you were not mistaken in the sentiments which I entertain for you or in my cordial sympathy with the Servian people. So long as the slightest hope exists of avoiding bloodshed all our efforts must be directed to that end. But if in spite of our earnest wish we are not successful, your Highness may rest assured that Russia will in no case disinterest herself in the fate of Servia."

When the Russian Minister in Belgrade read the Czar's reply to the Prime Minister of Servia, the Prime Minister embraced the Russian Minister and exclaimed, " The Czar is great and merciful."

The British Minister in St. Petersburg at the time was Sir George Buchanan. He was in constant touch with Sir Edward Grey at the Foreign Office. On July 25 he telegraphed to Sir Edward Grey as follows : " On my expressing earnest hope that Russia would not precipitate war by mobilising until you (Grey) have time to use your influence in favour of peace, His Excellency assured me that Russia had no aggressive intentions and she would take no action until it was forced on her.

" M. Cazanov added that Austria's action was in reality directed against Russia. He did not believe that Germany really wanted war, but her attitude was decided by ours. If we took our stand firmly with France and Russia there would be no war. If we failed them, new rivers of blood would flow and we would, in the end, be dragged into war."

Nevertheless, while the diplomats were talking throughout Europe, forces seemed to be driving towards the inevitability of war. Russia began mobilisation of her army. On July 29 the Czar sent an urgent message to the Kaiser, which read as follows :

" Am glad you're back. In this most serious moment I appeal to you to help me to try and avoid such a calamity as a European War ; I beg you, in the name of our old friendship, to stop your allies from going too far. Signed, Nicky."

Reading this telegram at his desk, the Kaiser scrawled across it, " A confession of his own weakness, and an attempt to put the responsibility on my shoulders."

On another document the Kaiser was writing : " I have no doubt left. England, France, and Russia have agreed among themselves to have the Austro-Servian conflict for an excuse for waging a war of extermination against us. Edward VII is stronger after death than I who am still alive, and there have been people who believe that England could still be won over or pacified by this or that puny measure ! "

On the night of July 24 Mr. Asquith, the Prime Minister, was writing this in his diary : " At 3.15 we had a Cabinet— the real interest was Grey's statement of the European situation, which is about as bad as it can possibly be. Austria has sent a bullying and humiliating ultimatum and demands an answer in forty-eight hours, failing which, she will march. This means almost inevitably that Russia will come on the scene, and, if so, it is difficult for both Germany and France to refrain from lending a hand. So that we are in measurable distance of a real Armageddon."

AN INTERESTING PICTURE *of King George at the Cenotaph for the* 1928 *Armistice
Day. It was on this occasion that he caught the chill which caused his serious illness.*

A BULLETIN *posted outside Buckingham Palace during King George's 1928 illness.*

NOVEMBER 1928 *was an anxious month for the nation. King George caught a chill at Sandringham, and his illness became serious. Crowds waited anxiously for the latest bulletins, which were posted up outside the Palace gates. A Council of Regency was appointed, consisting of the Queen, the Prince of Wales, the Primate, and the Prime Minister.*

WHEN KING GEORGE *had partly recovered from his illness, he was taken to Craigwell House, Bognor, to recuperate. Eventually he made a complete recovery.*

KING GEORGE *convalescing at Bognor.*

IN JULY 1929, AT WESTMINSTER ABBEY, *King George attended a Thanksgiving Service for his recovery from his serious illness.*

In the meantime France was offering her support to Russia, although all the ministers and diplomats in France seemed to be quite in the dark as to the attitude Britain would take in this rapidly approaching conflict.

Sir George Buchanan from St. Petersburg was sending more and more alarming messages. On one of these which he received Sir Edward Grey made the following annotation :

" Mr. Churchill told me to-day that the Fleet can be mobilised in twenty-four hours, but I think it is premature to make any statement to France and Russia yet."

Sunday, July 26, was an important day for the British Fleet. This is how Prince Louis of Battenburg, then First Sea Lord, describes it :

" The Fleet reassembled at Portsmouth was on the point of dispersing for demobilisation. The political outlook took an alarming turn by Austria's ultimatum to Servia. On the Sunday the Admiralty, as a precautionary measure, ordered the ships to remain where they were until further orders. For the moment Austria-Hungary, which had really provoked the diplomatic tangle by presenting Servia with an ultimatum and refusing to consider the acceptance in part of the Servian nation, seemed to be hesitating. No actual military move had yet been made."

On July 28 a formal declaration of war was sent by telegraph to the Servian Minister of Foreign Affairs from Vienna. It read : " The Royal Servian Government not having answered in a satisfactory manner the note of July 23 presented by the Austro-Hungarian Minister at Belgrade, the Imperial and Royal Government are themselves compelled to see to the safeguarding of their rights and interests, and with this object to have recourse to force of arms. Austria-Hungary consequently considers herself henceforward in a state of war with Servia."

Slowly, but surely and inevitably, Russia was proceeding with the mobilisation of her enormous army. The German Chief of Staff, Moltke, late on the night of the 30th, telegraphed to Conrad, the Austro-Hungarian Chief of Staff :

" Stand fast against Russian mobilisation. Austria-Hungary must be preserved. Mobilise at once against Russia. Germany will mobilise."

At about eight o'clock in the morning of July 23 mobilisation of the whole Austro-Hungarian Army was decided upon. The old Emperor Franz Josef signed the decree just after noon.

He telegraphed an hour later to the German Emperor : " In the consciousness of my grave obligation towards the future of my Empire I have ordered the mobilisation of my entire armed forces. I am aware of the full meaning and extent of my decision, at which I arrived with confidence in the justice of God, combined with the certainty that the strength of your defence will, with unflinching fidelity, furnish security for my Empire and for the Triple Alliance."

The German Emperor promptly replied :

" The preliminary mobilisation of my entire Army and Navy ordered by me to-day will be followed within the shortest period of time by actual mobilisation. I am reckoning on August 2 as the first day of mobilisation, and I am ready in fulfilment of the obligations of my alliance to commence war at once against Russia and France."

It now appeared that forces had been set in motion which nobody could stop. Despite the alarming reports of mobilisation everywhere in Europe, Sir Edward Grey was undoubtedly trying to save the situation. It was equally obvious that it had gone too far for it to stop.

France fully recognised that they were on the eve of a great conflict. The French Prime Minister had informed both St. Petersburg and London that " France is resolved to fulfil all the obligations of her alliance."

Sir Edward Grey asked the German Ambassador in London, Prince Lichnowsky, to call upon him. He told Prince Lichnowsky that if Germany could get any reasonable proposal put forward which made it clear that Germany and Austria were striving to preserve European peace, and that Russia and France would be unreasonable if they rejected it, he, Sir Edward Grey, would support it at St. Petersburg and Paris. He would also go to the length of saying that if Russia and France would not accept it, His Majesty's Government would have nothing more to do with the consequences. Otherwise Sir Edward Grey told the German Ambassador that, if France became involved, Britain would inevitably be drawn in.

A few hours later His Majesty King George V sent a last appeal to the Czar of Russia. Mr. Asquith describes this appeal in his diary.

It reads as follows : " A long message from Berlin to the effect that the German Ambassador's efforts for peace have been suddenly arrested and frustrated by the Czar's decree for a complete Russian mobilisation. We all set to work to draft a personal appeal from the King to the Czar. When we had settled it, I called a taxi and, in company with Tyrrell, drove to Buckingham Palace by about 1.30 a.m. The King was hauled out of his bed, and one of my strangest experiences was sitting with him, clad in a dressing-gown, while I read the message from Berlin and the proposed answer. The text was as follows : ' I cannot help thinking that some misunderstanding has produced this deadlock. I am most anxious not to miss any possibility of avoiding the terrible calamity which at present threatens the whole world. I therefore make a personal appeal to you.' "

The Czar promptly replied :

" I would gladly have accepted your proposal had not the German Ambassador this afternoon presented a note to my Government declaring war."

So Russia and Germany were definitely at war on the night of August 1. Germany had not waited for Russia's answer. At five o'clock that afternoon the Emperor Wilhelm had signed a decree mobilising the German Army. He signed it on a table made from the wood of the *Victory*, Nelson's flagship at Trafalgar. That night the Kaiser spoke thus to his people from the balcony of his Berlin castle :

" A fateful hour has fallen for Germany. Envious people everywhere are compelling us to our just defence. A sword has been forced into our hands. I hope that if my efforts at the last hour do not succeed in bringing our opponents to see eye to eye with us, and in maintaining peace, we shall, with God's help, so wield the sword that we shall restore it to its sheath again with honour.

" War will demand of us enormous sacrifices in property and life, but we

A BUST OF KING GEORGE *by Sir William Reid Dick, R.A.*

will show our enemies what it means to provoke Germany. And now I commend you to God. Go to church and kneel before God and pray for His help and for our gallant Army."

II

So far, the attitude of the British Government was still uncertain. There had been Cabinet meetings presided over by Mr. Asquith, in which the question of the neutrality of Belgium had been discussed. Britain was one of the signatories to that Treaty guaranteeing the independence of the country.

France had already declared to Britain that they would respect the neutrality of Belgium, and only in the event of some other Power violating the neutrality would France, in order to ensure defence of her own security, act otherwise.

It seemed certain, too, that France was about to be involved in this great conflict. France, in accordance with her Treaty obligations with Russia, began mobilising at 3.55 p.m. on August 1.

On August 2, very early, German troops began marching into Luxemburg. France was desperately anxious to know if Britain was going to stand by her. A Cabinet meeting had been held in Downing Street on the morning of Sunday, August 2, and a letter was read from Bonar Law, leader of the Conservative Opposition, agreeing to back up the Government in any measure they might take for the support of France and Russia.

That afternoon Sir Edward Grey received the French Ambassador and said : "I am authorised to give an assurance that if the German Fleet comes into the Channel or through the North Sea to undertake hostile operations against French coasts or shipping, the British Fleet will give all the protection in its power. This assurance is, of course, subject to the policy of His Majesty's Government receiving the support of Parliament, and must not be taken as binding."

The Cabinet again met in the evening, and came to a decision that if Belgian neutrality was violated, this country would declare war on Germany.

At 3 o'clock in the afternoon of Monday, August 3, Sir Edward Grey made a speech in a crowded House of Commons.

In a hushed and tense atmosphere he began his speech : " To-day events move so rapidly that it is exceedingly difficult to state with technical accuracy the actual state of affairs, but it is clear that the peace of Europe cannot be preserved. Russia and Germany at any rate have declared war upon each other.

" I now come to what we think the situation requires of us. For many years we have had a long-standing friendship with France. But how far that friendship entails obligation, let every man look into his own heart and his own feelings and construe the extent of the obligation for himself. I construe it myself as I feel it, but I do not wish to urge upon anyone else more than their feelings dictate as to what they should feel about the obligation.

" The House individually and collectively may judge for itself. I speak my personal view and I have given the House my own feeling in the matter. The French Fleet is now in the Mediterranean, and the northern and western

KING GEORGE *inspecting a guard of honour of Royal Marines on board H.M.S. Hood during his inspection of the Home Fleet at Weymouth in August 1932.*

coasts of France are absolutely unde-fended. The French Fleet being con-centrated in the Mediterranean, the situation is very different from that it used to be, because the friendship which has grown up between the two countries has given them a sense of security that there was nothing to be feared from us.

" My own feeling is that if a foreign fleet, engaged in a war which France has not sought and in which she has not been the aggressor, came down the English Channel and bombarded and battered the undefended coasts of France, we could not stand aside.

" I believe that would be the feeling of this country. We feel strongly that France is entitled to know—and to know at once—whether or not in the event of an attack upon her unprotected northern and western coasts, she could depend upon British support."

Sir Edward Grey then read the tele-gram from King Albert to King George. " Remembering the numerous proofs of your Majesty's friendship and that of your predecessor," telegraphed King Albert, " and the friendly attitude of England in 1870, and the proof of friendship you have just given us again, I make a supreme appeal for the diplo-matic intervention of your Majesty's Government to safeguard the integrity of Belgium."

Then Sir Edward Grey added: " If in a crisis, a time like this, we run away from these obligations of honour and interest as regards the Belgian Treaty, I doubt whether, whatever material force we might have at the end, it would be of very much value in place of the respect which we should have lost."

Just after Sir Edward Grey sat down he received a message from the Belgian Minister. Promptly he read it out :

" Germany sent yesterday evening at seven o'clock a note proposing to Bel-gium friendly neutrality covering free passage on Belgian territory, and promis-ing maintenance of independence of the kingdom and possession at the conclu-sion of peace, and threatening in case of refusal to treat Belgium as an enemy. A time limit of twelve hours is fixed for the reply.

" The Belgians have answered that an attack on their neutrality would be a flagrant violation of the rights of nations and that to accept the German proposal would be to sacrifice the honour of a nation. Conscious of its duty, Belgium is firmly resolved to repel aggression by all possible means. Of course I can only say that the Government are prepared to take into grave consideration the in-formation which it has received. I make no further comment upon it."

III

A dramatic scene ensued at the Foreign Office, in Whitehall. Night after night throughout this crisis lighted windows and hurrying couriers told of the excitement that raged within. Long despatches in code were being received from diplomats abroad.

Ministers in search of information were constantly on the telephone and interviewing the then Permanent Under-Secretary, Sir Arthur Nicolson.

The very small spy service then under control of the Foreign Office were send-ing their valuable reports. There is no doubt that the officials of the Foreign Office were fully aware of the trend of opinions in the various European countries, all of which showed a strong disposition for war.

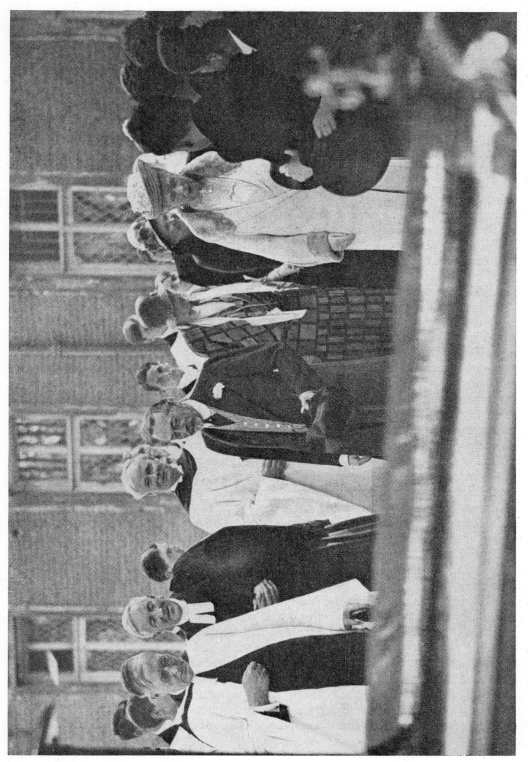

WHEN STAYING AT WINDSOR, *King George and Queen Mary frequently paid visits to Eton College, England's most fashionable Public School.*

While Sir Edward Grey was making his important speech in the House of Commons a group waited tensely to hear the result of that speech. At five o'clock in the evening Sir Arthur Nicolson was waiting in his room at the Foreign Office. A clerk burst in. He had been listening to the speech in the House of Commons.

" He has had a tremendous reception, sir," the clerk said. " The whole House was with him."

Sir Arthur Nicolson, weary with nights of vigil, rose from his chair.

" Thank God," he said. " Now the coast is clear. But it will be a terrible business."

Immediately the whole organisation of the Foreign Office began drafting out messages to be sent to the various Dominions and outposts of the Empire warning them that the British Empire was at war with Germany. Typewriters clattered, clerks scurried to and fro, codes were brought out from pigeon-holes, and those plans prepared well in advance for the use of our Consuls and Embassies abroad were immediately prepared in code for despatch abroad.

As this tremendous machinery was being set in motion Sir Edward Grey himself came into the room, and Sir Arthur Nicolson congratulated him on the success of his speech.

Sir Edward did not answer. He moved into the centre of the room and raised his clenched fists above his head. Then he brought his fist down with a crash upon the table.

" I hate war," he muttered. " I hate war."

At 8.30 that same evening Sir Edward Grey was still in the Foreign Office, conning the various despatches that were coming in from all over Europe. Twilight was sweeping across the whole of London. Sir Edward walked to the window and looked out.

" The lamps are going out all over Europe," he said. " We shall not see them lit again in our lifetime."

The Foreign Office received confirmation of the news that the Germans had entered Belgium and had announced that, if necessary, they would push their way through by force of arms.

These telegrams were rushed over to Downing Street, where Mr. Asquith was sitting with a Cabinet. After grave consideration of the reports, an ultimatum was drawn up by the British Cabinet and sent to the Germans, requesting them to give an assurance that they would respect Belgian neutrality. Otherwise the ultimatum would expire at midnight and the two countries would be at war.

Midnight in Germany meant 11 p.m. in England. So that only a few hours were left to know whether Germany and Britain would be at peace or at war.

Meantime the Foreign Office was working at full pressure. Countless electric lights blazed in every room. The great diplomatic plans for the event of the British Empire being at war were being put into operation. It necessitated immediate notification to all British representatives abroad, high and low, and for automatic telegraphic instructions regarding such necessities as the destruction of ciphers, the handing over of the protection of British subjects and interests to a neutral power, the departure of British officials from enemy countries, and other such matters.

The procedure to be followed had been most carefully worked out, elaborately enshrined in a sort of bible and entrusted for its execution to particularly efficient members of the staff. It

A HAPPY PICTURE *of King George chatting to some children.*

KING GEORGE'S *famous racing yacht*, Britannia.

KING GEORGE ABOARD HIS YACHT *BRITANNIA at Cowes.* *In the lower picture he is the figure on the farthest right.*

KING GEORGE *in genial mood.*

seemed that should war break out this machinery must work like clockwork.

And so, in fact, it did. Only the clock was fast, and here the Foreign Office made their one great mistake. Into a crowd of Foreign Office officials gathered in the corridors dashed a private secretary saying that Germany had declared war on England. This was not what was expected. Already a message had been typed and prepared which was to be sent to Prince Lichnowsky, the German Ambassador in London, at eleven o'clock that evening, announcing that the British Government had declared war on Germany.

In view of the report of the private secretary, this message was now altered. It was amended to " The German Empire having declared war upon Great Britain." This message was at once sent to Lichnowsky with his passport.

The Foreign Office messenger returned about 10.15. A few minutes later an urgent telegram arrived from Sir Edward Goschen at Berlin. It reported that the Chancellor had informed him by telephone that Germany would not reply to the ultimatum, and that therefore, to his infinite regret, a state of war would arise at midnight. Germany had, in fact, not declared war.

The Foreign Office realised that the mistake had been made, and that they had handed to Prince Lichnowsky an incorrect declaration of war. It was decided that at any cost this document must be retrieved and the right one substituted.

The youngest member of the Foreign Office staff was selected for this queer mission. It was Harold Nicolson, son of the Permanent Under-Secretary.

He walked across the Horse Guards Parade to the side door of the Embassy, at the bottom of the Duke of York's steps. After much ringing a footman appeared.

He stated that Prince Lichnowsky had gone to bed. The Foreign Office clerk stated that he was the bearer of a communication of the utmost importance from Sir Edward Grey. He was conducted to a room. There was a screen behind the door and behind the screen a vast bedstead, upon which the Ambassador was reclining in pyjamas.

The Foreign Office clerk stated that there had been a slight error in the document previously delivered, and that he had come to substitute for it another and more correct version.

Prince Lichnowsky indicated the writing-table in the window.

" You will find it there," he said.

A receipt had to be demanded and signed. A blotting-pad was brought across to the bed, and the pen dipped in the ink. While the Ambassador was signing, the sound of shouting came up from The Mall below, and the strains of the Marseillaise. The crowds were streaming back from Buckingham Palace.

The Great World War had begun. The wireless from the Admiralty was already cackling its warning messages to the British Fleet scattered over the seven seas.

A QUIET DAY'S RACING *at Newbury.*

KING GEORGE *congratulating his trainer, W. Jarvis, after the victory of his horse Limelight in the Newbury Spring Cup.*

A CHARACTERISTIC STUDY.

KING GEORGE *inspecting the Guard of Honour when arriving in Scotland for his annual holiday at Balmoral Castle.*

KING GEORGE *at the Trooping of the Colour.*

WORLD ECONOMIC CONFERENCE. *Sixty-five nations sent representatives to the World Economic Conference, which opened at the Geological Museum, South Kensington, on June 12, 1933. It was held to find means of ending the world trade depression, but no solution was reached. Here King George is seen at the inauguration ceremony.*

AN INFORMAL STUDY of *Princess Elizabeth, who is now second in line of succession to the Throne.*

PRINCESS ELIZABETH *with her young sister, Princess Margaret Rose.*

KING GEORGE AND QUEEN MARY *with their granddaughter Princess Elizabeth.*

KING GEORGE AND QUEEN MARY AT ALDERSHOT, *followed by their daughter and son-in-law, and their two grandsons.*

ism and self-sacrifice which they have displayed in raising by voluntary enlistment, since the commencement of the War, no less than 5,041,000 men, an effort far surpassing that of any other nation in similar circumstances recorded in history, and one which will be a lasting source of pride to future generations."

A few days later, on May 31, came the naval battle off the coast of Jutland. In reply to a birthday message from Admiral Jellicoe on behalf of the Grand Fleet, the King wrote that he was deeply touched, and added :

" It reached me on the morrow of a battle which has once more displayed the splendid gallantry of the officers and men under your command.

" I mourn the loss of brave men, many of them personal friends of my own, who have fallen in their country's cause. Yet even more do I regret that the German High Sea Fleet, in spite of its heavy losses, was enabled by the misty weather to evade the full consequences of an encounter they have always professed to desire, but for which when the opportunity arrived they showed no inclination."

Early in June the King visited the Grand Fleet, and addressed representatives of its various units on parade.

II

The 4th of August saw the beginning of the third year of the War, and was marked by every possible sign of resolve of the whole Empire to persevere until complete and final victory was attained. The King fittingly expressed the national determination in a message dated " Midnight, August 3," addressed to the Heads and Sovereigns of Allied States and in another to the King of the Belgians, in which he expressed the assurance of his confidence, " that the united efforts of the Allies will liberate Belgium from the oppression of her aggressors and will restore to her the full enjoyment of her national and economic independence.

" I would also desire to convey to Your Majesty my deep sympathy in the grievous trials to which Belgium has been so unjustly subjected, and which she has borne with such admirable fortitude."

To the Sovereigns and Heads of the Allied States he wrote :

" On this day, the second anniversary of the great conflict in which my country and her gallant Allies are engaged, I desire to convey to you my steadfast resolution to prosecute the war until our united efforts have attained the objects for which we have in common taken up arms.

" I feel assured that you are in accord with me in the determination that the sacrifices which our valiant troops have so nobly made shall not have been offered in vain, and that the liberties for which they are fighting shall be fully guaranteed and secured."

Meanwhile, in July, the King had sent a cheering message to Sir Douglas Haig :

" I am proud of my troops ; none could have fought more bravely." And in August he paid another notable visit, which lasted a week, to the Army in France. On this occasion the King saw everything with his own eyes— trenches, captured dug-outs, batteries, and prisoners ; his days were spent most strenuously, and his presence was most heartily appreciated by the soldiers. How deeply impressed he was by all that he saw was reflected afterwards by the approval he gave to the " Battle of the Somme " films—" the public," he said, " should see the pictures, that they may have some idea of what the Army is doing and what it means." On the conclusion of his visit he issued a General Order, which, though restrained in language, bore many traces of real emotion :

" I have realised (he said) not only the splendid work which has been done in immediate touch with the enemy—in the air, underground, as well as on the ground—but also the vast organisations behind the fighting line, honourable alike to the genius of the initiators and to the heart and hand of the workers. Everywhere there is proof that all men and women are playing their part, and I rejoice to think their noble efforts are being heartily seconded by all classes at home.

" Do not think that I and your fellow-countrymen forget the heavy sacrifices which the Armies have made and the bravery and endurance they have displayed during the past two years of bitter conflict. These sacrifices have not been in vain ; the arms of the Allies will never be laid down until our cause has triumphed."

The King had done untold good to the Army by not allowing himself to be dissuaded from taking the risks of the battlefield. With no shadow of disrespect, thousands of soldiers were talking of him as " a real sport." His messages at Christmas to the soldiers and sailors spoke of his " grateful thoughts," " for victories gained, for hardships endured, and for your unfailing cheeriness." " The Empire,"

he added, " confident in you, remains determined to win."

Confidence and determination had struck the note of his speech proroguing Parliament a day or two before, and were to strike that of his New Year's Message to the President of the French Republic and of his Speech on the reassembling of Parliament in February 1917.

In July that year he and the Queen visited France and Belgium for ten days ; it was the first time for six centuries that the King and Queen of England had been at a seat of war together. For the King it was his fourth visit to the Front, and once more the special order which he issued on its conclusion bore witness to the fineness of his sensibility and to the nobility of his temperament.

It was at this stage in the War that the King took a step which gave unqualified satisfaction throughout the British Dominions. He abolished all German titles and dignities in the Royal Family, and assumed the family name of Windsor. The style of " Royal Highness " was restricted in future to all children of the Sovereign and to his grandchildren in the male line only. The titles of " Prince " and " Princess " were similarly limited.

III

" At least the King is doing without his beer," was the remark many a soldier blurted out during the War when groups of men were apt to discuss the shortcomings of those people safely entrenched in high circles in London.

That spontaneous gesture of King

LAUNCHING QUEEN MARY, September 1934. The Queen christened and launched Queen Mary, the world's largest liner, on September 26, 1934, at Clydebank before 250,000 people. King George accompanied her at the ceremony.

THE GREAT EVENT of 1934 was the wedding of H.R.H. the Duke of Kent, King George's youngest son, to Princess Marina of Greece. They became engaged whilst they were on holiday.

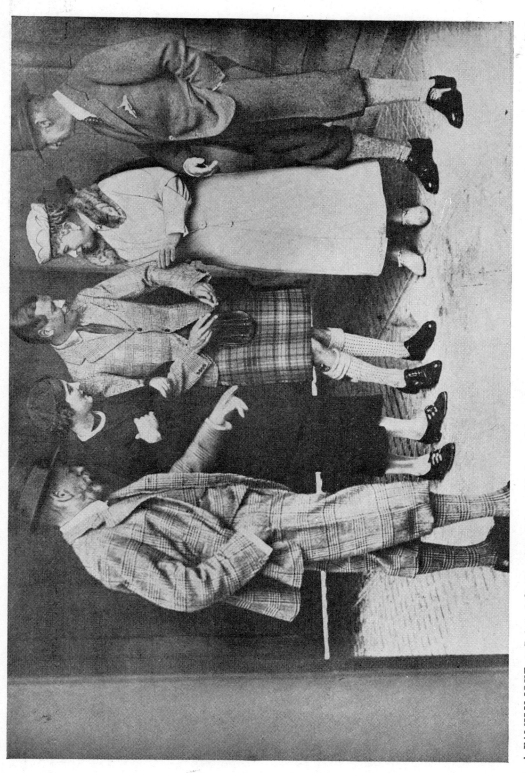

A FAMILY JOKE at Balmoral Castle, where Princess Marina and her parents went to stay with King George and Queen Mary where her engagement to the Duke of Kent was announced.

THE ROYAL WEDDING. *The scene in Westminster Abbey when the Duke of Kent and Princess Marina were married on November 29, 1934.*

THE ROYAL WEDDING. *Thousands gathered outside Buckingham Palace to cheer the bride and bridegroom. The top picture shows them acknowledging the cheers. Below: King George holding up little Princess Margaret Rose to wave to the crowd.*

A FAMILY GROUP *taken after the wedding of the Duke and Duchess of Kent.*

George during the War was one that appealed to the individual soldier. It gave him to understand that Royalty was prepared to set an example to others. But King George, as also the Prince of Wales, did much more during those years than forgo little luxuries. They placed themselves with the Army, in France and Flanders.

Not only that, but the King visited the Grand Fleet at frequent intervals, and we are told that on many naval matters his advice was eagerly sought. From the beginning to the end of hostilities no naval manœuvre or move was outside his knowledge, and few took place without their being the subject of his well-judged comments.

And so it was with the Army. Every new invention and new suggestion for the equipment or comfort of the men in the line or the precise field strength in each theatre of war were subjects on which he demanded close and constant information.

On frequent occasions during the War, Royal visits were paid to important factories and workshops at the munitions centres throughout Britain, as well as to shipbuilding yards, hospitals, and other institutions engaged in war work of one kind or another.

Early in the War the Prince of Wales was eager to take his place on the Western Front. He wanted no easy and safe job at the base, but because he was Heir to the Throne it was insisted that he be attached to General Headquarters.

Even so, constant watchfulness by those responsible for the safety of the Prince did not prevent him from escaping into the battle zones again and again. On many occasions he was under fire, and was able to prove himself. He early displayed an unusual and able

interest in military tactics, and was able to study the military operations from the beginning to the end.

After a period of apprenticeship at G.H.Q., the Prince succeeded in getting posted to the Staff of the Guards Division.

This was not quite what he wanted. He would have liked to have commanded a platoon and gone over the top at the head of his men, but as he could not attain his heart's desire he settled down to really hard work on the " Q " side—that is, in the branch of Divisional Headquarters controlled by the Assistant Quartermaster-General, who is responsible for the quarters and general comfort of the troops.

The Prince was appointed Staff Captain of the Mediterranean Expeditionary Force in 1916 and promoted D.A.Q.M.G. in the same year. He attained his twenty-fifth birthday in 1915, whilst serving in the field, but naturally that year was not a time for any sort of public rejoicing, and the event passed almost unnoticed.

The Prince came in for a useful sphere of activity during the winter of 1915–1916, when the British Government appointed a National Committee to make permanent provision for the care of British graves in France and Belgium. The Prince was appointed President of this new body and took an active interest in its important duties.

There was no lack of work for the Prince, but it must be admitted that during the whole of his service on the French Front his complete disregard of personal danger continued to be a constant source of anxiety, and, popular as he was with all ranks, it was with a sigh of something like relief that the High

Command witnessed his departure from France.

Subsequently the Prince visited the Italian Front, and took with him that same keenness and interest in military operations. Thus, by the time the Armistice came, the Prince of Wales had a wider experience of war than any man of his generation.

IV

The King's activities continued to be essentially public enterprises, even when they appeared to bear a more private character. The War, in its minor operations, as well as its major, was never for a moment out of his thoughts, and when the fateful year 1918 dawned after a depressing autumn, and with the prospects of yet darker events ahead, the King continued to express the spirit of the whole Empire, in the same terms of calm courage and steadfast resolution.

If Russia had not been able to persevere, the entry of the United States, followed by that of other neutral States, had united practically the whole of the civilised world ; and, until a recognition was offered by Germany of the only principles on which an honourable peace could be concluded, it was our duty to prosecute the War with all the vigour that we possessed. Sombre days, as all will remember, soon set in, and towards the end of this March, after the first devastating German attack, the King visited once more the Western Front.

His letter written to Sir Douglas Haig, after his return, bore witness to the fierceness of the battle still raging,

the "indomitable courage and unflinching tenacity with which my splendid troops have withstood the supreme effort of the greater part of the enemy's fighting power."

He commended, too, the speed with which casualty clearing stations were enabled to carry out their work ; and it so happened that his next public document related to the Red Cross, for it was a letter congratulating *The Times* on the immense total—£10,000,000—which had then been raised for the needs of the Joint War Committee's Fund, and which was afterwards largely exceeded.

In May he reviewed a regiment of the United States National Army at Buckingham Palace ; and to each officer and man there had been given on disembarkation a facsimile of his Message of Welcome, dated Windsor Castle, April 1918, in the following words :

" Soldiers of the United States, the people of the British Isles welcome you on your way to take your stand beside the Armies of Many Nations now fighting in the Old World the great battle for human freedom.

" The Allies will gain new heart and spirit in your company. I wish I could shake the hand of each one of you and bid you God-speed on your mission."

The " great battle," if we apply that word more particularly to the continuous fighting of the last months of the War, had already passed its crisis and begun to swing irrevocably in the Allies' favour, when in July the King and Queen celebrated their Silver Wedding.

The occasion was purposely shorn of

LORD WIGRAM, *the King's private secretary and personal friend. It was to him that King George put his touching death-bed question, " How is the Empire ? "*

KING GEORGE AND QUEEN MARY *spent several weeks at Eastbourne early in* 1935, *where they occupied the Duke of Devonshire's house. The top photograph shows the crowd which gathered when the King and Queen walked on the front, and the bottom one was taken after a visit to the parish church.*

elaborate ceremony ; but there was a visit to the City, a special service in St. Paul's, and at the Guildhall a presentation to the King by the Lord Mayor, on behalf of the citizens, of a cheque for £53,000 to be devoted to such charities as the King might desire.

The King acknowledged the gift in a fine speech, in the course of which he referred with joyful gratitude to the " wholehearted response to the call of duty which had reverberated through the Empire "; to his admiration, based on what he had seen, of our fleets and our armies, and to the comradeship of war in which he rejoiced that he and the Queen and their children had been able to bear part.

At last, on November 11, the fighting was over ; and it fell to the King to express without the impending shadow of more slaughter, but happily and finally, the faith which had always been in him from the first day of the War. To the Navy his message went :

" Ever since that fateful Fourth of August, 1914, I have remained steadfast in my confidence that, whether fortune frowned or smiled, the Royal Navy would once more prove the sure shield of the British Empire in the hour of trial.

" Never in its history has the Royal Navy, with God's help, done greater things for us, nor better sustained its old glories and the chivalry of the seas.

" With full and grateful hearts, the peoples of the British Empire salute the White, the Red, and the Blue Ensigns, and those who have given their lives for the Flag.

" I am proud to have served in the Navy. I am prouder still to be its head on this memorable day."

The King's address to " all the ranks of the Army of the British Empire, Home, Dominion, Colonial, and Indian Troops " contained the following triumphant passage :

" Soldiers of the British Empire ! In France and Belgium the prowess of your arms, as great in retreat as in victory, has won the admiration alike of friend and foe, and has now by a happy historic fate enabled you to conclude the campaign by capturing Mons, where your predecessors of 1914 shed the first British blood. Between that date and then you have traversed a long and weary road ; defeat has more than once stared you in the face ; your ranks have been thinned again and again by wounds, sickness, and death ; but your faith has never faltered, your courage has never failed, your hearts have never known defeat."

In congratulating the Air Force he declared that :

" Our aircraft have been ever in the forefront of the battle ; pilots and observers have constantly maintained the offensive throughout the ever-changing fortunes of the day, and in the war zones our gallant dead have lain always beyond the enemies' lines or far out to sea.

" The birth of the Royal Air Force, (he continued) with its wonderful expansion and development, will ever remain one of the most remarkable achievements of the Great War."

It is well to recall these utterances, for the King was far more than their mere official mouthpiece. Even if we were so frigid as to attempt to rule out the personality of the Monarch who was speaking, the historic fact would yet remain that no Sovereign upon earth had ever had occasion to address his sailors and soldiers in such a strain before, to congratulate so many men under arms, to speak for so many parts of the globe's surface, to view in mind the conclusion of so gigantic a conflict. The position in which King George V found himself on Armistice Day was without parallel in the records of monarchy anywhere, and will probably remain for all time unique.

Naturally, in the celebrations which ensued, the King was the leading figure. On Armistice Day, the King, the Queen and other members of the Royal Family were spontaneously and enthusiastically greeted as they appeared before immense crowds which had congregated about Buckingham Palace.

On the following day they attended in state the Service of Thanksgiving at St. Paul's ; and a week later the King sent an inspiring message to his people in reply to addresses from both Houses of Parliament.

In the Royal Gallery in the Pale of Westminster, amid Lords and Commons and distinguished representatives of the Dominions and of India, he paid warm tribute to the work of the Forces and their commanders, to the contributions of the Dominions and of India, and to the efforts of the Allies.

He called for the creation of a better Britain, and for the preservation of the spirit of comradeship which had been shown in the years of the War. It was perhaps the longest allocution that the King ever delivered ; and it concluded with an exhortation characteristic of the man, for, looking back upon the turbulent and perilous past, it summoned men's thoughts to the fresh duties which lay immediately before them.

As a sailor, the King made haste to visit his victorious Fleet, and the next day saw him travelling north to Rosyth, where in the harbour and beyond it vessels of all types dressed ship to do him honour.

The whole of the Grand Fleet was inspected ; at one point the American vessels were on the starboard and British vessels on the port, and there was no distinguishing the heartiness of the greeting from each side.

Hardly was this visit over when a less formal greeting was to salute the King and Queen, as the King reviewed in Hyde Park a great army of men wearing the Silver Badge for Services Rendered.

In a frenzy of loyalty, so spontaneous as to be almost embarrassing, the Silver Badge men swarmed round the King's open carriage, forgetting for the moment all sense of discipline in their uncontrollable desire to shake hands with the object of their devotion.

France was the next scene, and it was evident that there also the King would meet with a rousing reception. He arrived, with the Prince of Wales and Prince Albert, in Paris, on November 28 ; and it was believed that never had such a vast concourse assembled in the French capital before.

The King and the Princes had spent the night at British Headquarters, and were received on their arrival by President Poincaré. The procession that was formed rode through the streets in high triumph, and everything was most happily symbolical of the union of the two nations.

At the banquet in the evening the King recalled in his speech the desperate efforts of German armies against Paris, and " the skilful direction and strategy of the distinguished Field-Marshal Foch."

On the following day he was received, on an occasion of even greater popular

KING GEORGE *out riding in the Row, Hyde Park, in* 1935.

HER MAJESTY QUEEN MARY. *A portrait taken during Jubilee year.*

H.M. KING GEORGE V. *A portrait taken during Jubilee year.*

KING GEORGE'S FOUR SONS—EDWARD VIII, THE DUKE OF YORK, THE
DUKE OF GLOUCESTER, AND THE DUKE OF KENT.

THE DUCHESS OF YORK *with her daughters, Princesses Elizabeth and Margaret Rose.*
The elder daughter is now second in line of succession to the throne.

enthusiasm, by the Municipal Council of Paris, and the climax to his official visit to the French came fittingly when he conferred on Marshal Foch the Order of Merit.

From Paris he set out for the Western Front, where he received a glad welcome from the British Armies, visited battlefields which had only recently been won back from the enemy, and entered the long-tried city of Lille.

Among the soldiers he moved often in an informal manner on foot, and was everywhere the object of an affectionate following. Such may be said to have been the culmination of the King's war services, and to him, as to all who had served under him, the winter of 1918 marked the principal stage of a lifetime.

One of the last official acts of the King that year was to receive President Wilson in London on his arrival in Europe for the Peace Settlement.

CHAPTER VII

THE GREAT SLUMP

King George's private life—His stamp collection—Horse-racing—Tours abroad—
A constitutional monarch.

I

THOSE years of war effort took their toll upon the health of King George. Although some years were to pass before the first real serious illness developed, it was obvious that His Majesty emerged from that great conflict an old man.

But, as was emphasised at the beginning of this record of his life, there was to be no rest for him, no retirement from the onerous duties of State until death came to him at Sandringham.

In fact, the years immediately following upon the Armistice were to make even greater demands upon the rapidly ageing King. A new world was in the making, and the head of the State had to play an important part. What most people did not realise was that an even greater ordeal lay before Britain in the near future—years of economic disaster, falling currencies, crushing debt, and the Great Slump.

At the moment, however, there was a sort of hysterical relief that the Armistice had brought to an end years of bloody warfare. Money was plentiful, and there was a general expectation that the Allied victory would bring a wealth of loot to Paris, Rome, New York, and London. The mass of the people thankfully doffed their uniforms and hurried back to the workaday world.

It was left to politicians, diplomats, and war-weary statesmen to concoct that fantastic document of peace known as the Treaty of Versailles. Perhaps it would have been better if the ordinary man in the street had paid more attention to international politics at that time. But he was more concerned with the problems of his own bread-and-butter existence. The scramble for jobs had begun. The scramble for world territories, mandates, and the like, were left to the statesmen.

King George was in a difficult position. His advice was always ready to be given—if requested. But it has to be admitted that those who made the Peace rarely consulted the man whose wide experience and knowledge of statecraft would have been of incalculable value.

But, in the topsy-turveydom of war, monarchies on the Continent were more than suspect. The Kaiser had abdicated and fled to Holland. A former journalist, Mussolini, had arisen in Italy, and by means of his powerful personality overshadowed the existence of the King of Italy. Turkey had sent the last of the rulers of that unfortunate country packing, and one, Mustapha Kemal, had appointed himself Dictator. Statesmen eyed uneasily these new experiments in Government.

To King George, therefore, was left

the dull but exacting round of ceremonial duties. He continued his task with that same close devotion to duty that had marked all his actions since coming to the Throne. During these years and until his illness the King's routine of work was not surpassed in strenuousness by any of his ministers. His regular routine, when in London, is well worth recording.

He got up each day at 7.20 a.m. Before eight he was at work in his study. After a brief interval for breakfast, he was at work again before ten o'clock. He worked solidly till luncheon, with a break of forty minutes, during which he would walk briskly in the garden of the Palace with the Equerry on duty. This was the only opportunity for air and exercise which he took all day.

He was at work again from 2.30 to 5 p.m. Almost invariably he dined *tête-à-tête* with the Queen, and the evening passed in reading current literature or perhaps pursuing his hobby of philately.

It may be asked what State business called for such tremendous application. The answer is found partly in the list of major political events which fell during this period, and partly in the King's interpretation of his duties and responsibilities.

He felt that on every State question he must form his own unfettered judgment. To that end, he forbade the marking of State documents by ministers and officials and he refused to read précis. He felt that he alone could be the judge of what was relevant to his own decisions. It was his habit also to read his daily paper almost from cover to cover.

Of such little leisure as was left to him, he made the best use. His simple, homely tastes emphasised the true democracy of this King of the greatest of all world democracies.

Only in the royal home, as distinct from the Royal Household, was the light that beats upon the Throne really turned off. Only at home did the King and Queen enjoy some measure of the privacy which is the common possession, almost the Divine right, of their people.

The home life of Their Majesties was wholly isolated from the pomp and circumstance of the Court. It was quietly spent in the seclusion of the strictly private apartments of the Royal Family, whether in Buckingham Palace or in Windsor Castle—a little oasis of cosy domesticity set in a wilderness of spacious salons, wide floors, high ceilings, approached by stately and cold marble staircases.

Their Majesties lived a homely life. Society did not greatly appeal to them, nor company either. Queen Mary is the most domesticated of women, a true housewife.

Perhaps the truest picture of the Royal home life is one which presents the King, at rest after a hard and trying day over State affairs, reading the latest book of travel or biography to the Queen, while Her Majesty is engaged with busy fingers on crochet for charitable gifts.

In former times the King or Queen was allowed hardly a moment of privacy. Sleeping or waking, dressing or undressing, eating or drinking, walking or sitting, indoors or out of doors, there was always some Court functionary, male or female, in close attendance from whom there was no escape.

At home, King George and Queen Mary saw to it that they were untroubled by the attentions of Gold Stick

LONDON *had never before seen such loyal demonstrations as were given to King George and Queen Mary during their Jubilee State Drive through the streets of the Empire's capital on May 6,* 1935.

LOOKING DOWN *on the amazing scene in Trafalgar Square, where thousands waited for hours to see the drive in State to St. Paul's Cathedral.*

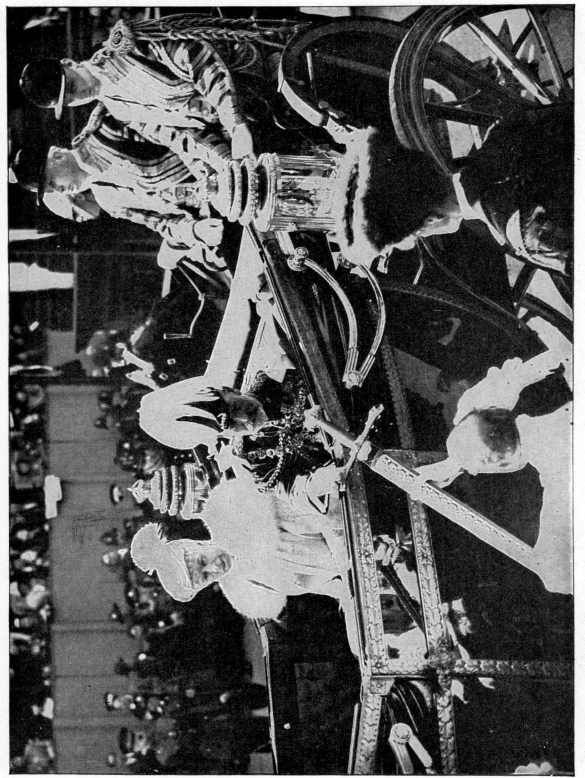

KING GEORGE, *wearing the uniform of a Field-Marshal, halting at Temple Bar in his drive with the Queen to St. Paul's Cathedral to receive the historic Pearl Sword from the Lord Mayor in token of the City's homage.*

KING GEORGE AND QUEEN MARY, *with members of their family and their officers of State, during the Thanksgiving Service in St. Paul's Cathedral. An Address was given by the Archbishop of Canterbury, and the entire service was broadcast throughout the British Empire.*

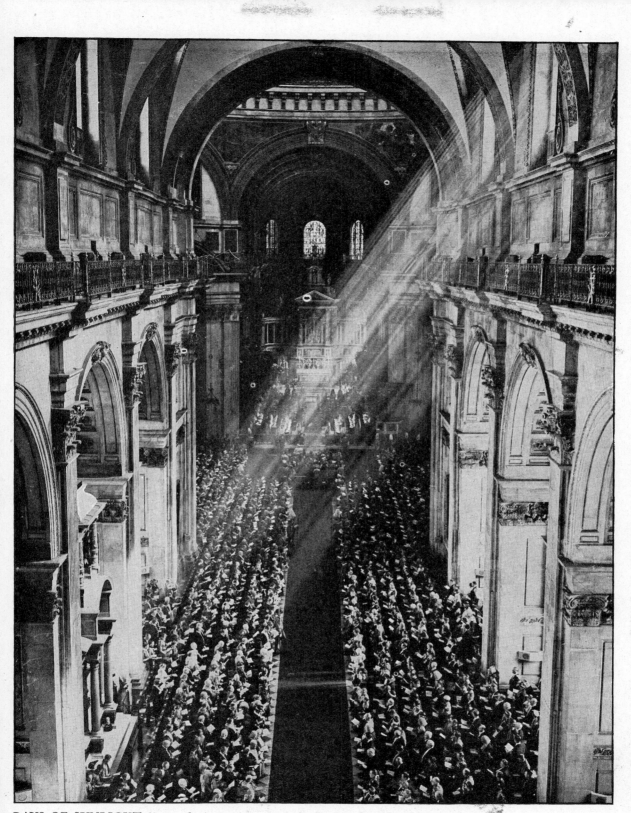

RAYS OF SUNLIGHT *lit up the impressive scene in St. Paul's, where the leading citizens of the Empire gave thanks for the continued reign of their King.*

AFTER THE DRIVE back to Buckingham Palace, King George and Queen Mary and their family came out on to the balcony to acknowledge the cheers of nearly 200,000 people. "My very dear people . . . the Queen and I thank you from the bottom of our hearts for all the loyalty . . . and love with which . . . you have surrounded us," said the King in a broadcast to the Empire.

THE JUBILEE *was celebrated by rich and poor in every part of the country, and houses were decorated with flags and bunting. In Palace Road, in the East End of London,* **a tea was** *given to the poor children of the district.*

LONDON was floodlit during the Jubilee celebrations, and several hundred thousand people thronged the streets every night. Traffic was banned in certain areas because of the crowds at nighteen. This photograph shows Buckingham Palace lit up by floodlights.

in Waiting, or Silver Stick in Waiting, or even Silver Stick Adjutant in Waiting. Whatever service they required was supplied by their own domestic servants.

It was at Sandringham that their Majesties' hearts were set and their first fond hopes remained—Sandringham, their country seat, as it was the country seat of King Edward and Queen Alexandra before them.

It is one of the best sporting estates in the country. About 10,000 pheasants are reared there annually. There is an entire absence of warnings, so familiar elsewhere, as to prosecution for trespass and pains and penalties. But the King's preserves are never poached. This is to be attributed more to the loyalty of poachers than to the vigilance of keepers.

King George's favourite sport was game-shooting. As a shot he had very few equals. It is doubtful whether any adept at the gun could do much more than hold his own with the King at driven birds. Many stories are told of his fine shooting. One relates to grouse at Balmoral.

The King with his two guns was in a butt towards which eleven driven grouse came flying, but on reaching the butt the birds turned and crossed the line. Nevertheless, the King brought down four of the birds in front of the butt, and four behind—a feat in shooting with two guns which, for rapidity and precision, it would be difficult to beat. In pheasant-shooting at Sandringham, the King's average of successes was over 80 per cent. of the cartridges fired.

To be so good an all-round shot as King George requires uncommon steadiness of nerve, quickness and accuracy of vision. These qualities can only be secured by simple and plain living and regular exercise throughout the year. His Majesty was probably the most temperate and abstemious King that has ever sat on the English Throne. Walking was the form of exercise he preferred. He liked it better even than riding.

His ability as a shot is common knowledge. He really was in his time one of the twelve best shots in Britain. It was popular belief that he used an old-fashioned gun with hammers. Actually the hammers were dummies, used for sighting purposes. Queerly enough, he usually shot wearing a red tie.

On one occasion in Norfolk he shot a jay, an attractive bird, but a nuisance where other birds' eggs are concerned. He happened to overhear a young woman who was watching say, " I wish I could get that jay which the King shot." He had it sent to her with a charming message.

Of his hobby of collecting stamps, these things can be said :

He began to collect when he was a boy.

He had every issued stamp of the British Empire.

The value of his collection was fabulous.

A special " stamp man " was regularly employed to look after his stamps, which were on boards, not in albums. The collection was kept in Buckingham Palace, and when in London the King gave an hour a day to his stamps, if he could spare the time. He really did like stamps, but no one else in his family took much interest in them.

If possible, the King liked to go to bed about 10.30. Whenever he went to the theatre, the management concerned was always at great pains to get the curtain down promptly to time. This time problem was always a big one when the King and Queen went to "Command" variety shows. Artists were inclined to make the most of their opportunity and to go on longer than they were scheduled.

If and when this happened and the programme overran, police arrangements about street traffic were upset, and the servants at Buckingham Palace were kept up late—which did not please the King. He was thoughtful about his servants.

The King's hearing in later years was not too good, and at these Royal variety shows an unobtrusive amplifier was installed in the Royal box. Partly on account of this difficulty, he liked visual turns—acrobats and such like—better than vocal turns.

His favourite actor was Henry Ainley; his favourite comedian George Robey. In some ways this was because Ainley and Robey had voices which reached him without his having to strain to hear them. His favourite film star latterly was Grace Moore; his favourite actress Edith Day, in "Rose Marie."

During the lifetime of King Edward VII it was considered fitting that the racing interests of the Royal Family should be nominally centred in the King. Thus it was that King George did not own racehorses until his accession to the Throne, though he had previously attended many meetings and in other ways had manifested more than a passing interest in what is sometimes called "The Sport of Kings."

Race-goers were rejoiced to know soon after his Accession that His Majesty had decided to continue his father's stable at Egerton House, together with the important stud farm at Sandringham.

To the present generation of racing people the Derby of 1913 is much the most memorable of any race, not only because of the disqualification of Craganour, but also because of the tragic interference with the King's colt Anmer.

Emily Davison, a Suffragist fanatic, rushed out from beneath the rails near Tattenham Corner and endeavoured to clutch the horse, which in falling so badly injured the woman that she died a few days later

His Majesty did not attend a race meeting during the War, but continued to run his horses. In March 1916, the King presented Anmer to the Canadian Government for remount breeding.

Success in a Classic event was denied to the Royal colours until the season of 1928, when Scuttle won the One Thousand Guineas. This victory was all the more pleasing to His Majesty as the filly was bred at Sandringham.

It was a great public disappointment when Scuttle failed to win the Oaks, in which she ran second to the Earl of Derby's Toboggan.

Several of the chief handicaps were won by horses in the Royal stables, Weathervane scoring a highly popular triumph in the Royal Hunt Cup at Ascot in 1923. London Cry was another useful performer, winning the Goodwood Stakes and the Prince Edward Handicap. His Majesty won five races in 1928 of the total value of £9,565.

In 1929, Lyme Regis secured the valuable Prince of Wales's Stakes for three-year-olds at Ascot, and Magnum Bonum—a great favourite—was successful in three long-distance handicaps.

STAMPS *which were issued to celebrate King George's Silver Jubilee.*

DURING THE JUBILEE CELEBRATIONS *King George and Queen Mary made State drives through all parts of London. Wherever they went they were received with remarkable scenes of loyalty and devotion.*

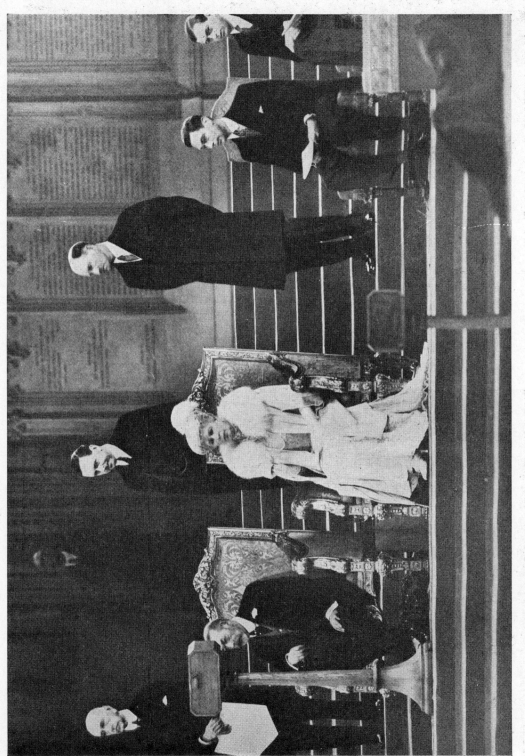

KING GEORGE AT WESTMINSTER HALL, *to receive addresses of congratulation from Parliament on attaining his Silver Jubilee. In replying, the King made touching references to the help which had been given him by " my dear wife."*

KING GEORGE'S *last visit to Epsom to see the Derby, in June* 1935.

A ROYAL VISIT TO ASCOT.

KING GEORGE at the last Trooping of the Colour which he ever attended.

17

The total amount won in stakes was £4,480. The season of 1930 was an uneventful one, Fairy Story and Patrick being the only successful bearers of the Royal colours.

Major Featherstonhaugh, who had taken Lord Marcus Beresford's place as manager of the King's stud and racing stable, died in 1931, and was succeeded in that position in the following year by Brigadier H. A. Tomkinson, in his day an international polo player.

Mr. W. R. Jarvis had followed Mr. Richard Marsh as trainer at Egerton House, and one of the best horses he had there was Limelight, who, bred at Sandringham, was a son of Pharos. At Ascot he won the Jersey Stakes and the Hardwicke Stakes, his other successes including the Duke of York Handicap, under a big weight, the Newbury Spring Cup, and the Prince of Wales's Nursery at Doncaster. After winning £8,900 in stakes, Limelight was retired to the Sandringham Stud.

All Limelight's victories were gained under heavy weights, and the King's affection for the horse prompted a last visit to Limelight's box.

King George took great interest in all the sports which appeal to his subjects, but yachting was his chief delight. This was natural in a former " Sailor Prince," who never lost his love of the sea.

Cowes Regatta, which he invariably attended with the Queen, was his principal holiday of the year, and during the famous week he enjoyed himself to the utmost.

His first yacht was the cutter *Corisande*, which he bought from the Duke of Leeds, but it was not until he inherited the famous racing cutter *Britan-nia* from King Edward that he took up yacht-racing in earnest.

But the time came when the forty-two-year-old *Britannia* could not compete with modern yachts. Last season, for the first time, she did not win a race. The King decided to give up this royal sport. It was a great wrench to part with *Britannia*, and he would not think of racing any other vessel.

II

It can be said that this disarming simplicity of King George gave no indication to the statesmen of the world of the deep affection and loyalty with which he was regarded by his millions of subjects. Not until the Silver Jubilee celebrations were the eyes of these blind men opened. Then, the cheering millions, the enthusiastic scenes, the daily demonstrations proved that even statesmen may not know wherein the real affection of the people lay.

The triumph of Armistice Day in 1918, when thousands of his subjects thronged the approaches to Buckingham Palace and sent up to the King and Queen standing upon the balcony what those who heard it can only describe as a stupendous roar of heartfelt welcome, remained for the rest of his days an imperishable memory.

The scene which followed when, led by the Guards' band, that vast assemblage sang solemnly and reverently " Land of Hope and Glory " will remain for all time one of the classic moments of English history long after the last participator therein has followed the monarch to the grave.

In the capital of our French Allies a few weeks later, King George and his

Consort received another ovation as overwhelming and spontaneous. But in no public ceremony connected with the War was King George more his true, kindly, unaffected self than as chief mourner representing the nation at the bier of Britain's Unknown Warrior and at the graveside in Westminster Abbey.

On January 18, 1919, Their Majesties were saddened by the death of their youngest son, Prince John.

On February 19 the King attended a memorial service in Westminster Abbey to the officers and men of the Royal Air Force who had fallen in the War, and at the end of July he received in Buckingham Palace deputations from public bodies who had come to present addresses of congratulation on the successful issue of the War. He took this opportunity of reminding his hearers of social reforms that still awaited fulfilment.

" We cannot but remember with heartfelt gratitude all those who have offered up their lives as a willing sacrifice, and those others who, wounded and disabled, have suffered for us. Well may we repeat, ' With a great sum attained we this freedom.'

" For their sake we are bound to regard the conclusion of Peace not as a call to rest or relaxation, but as a stimulus to new and greater efforts."

On July 19 the military celebrations of the victory were held in London. There was a march past of troops representing all the Allies, the salute being taken by the King at the base of the Queen Victoria Memorial.

On July 29 His Majesty visited the City—and delivered a stirring speech on the mighty tasks—that could be made magnificent tasks—which lay before the capital of the Empire.

In October 1919 the King sent a message to the inaugural meeting of the League of Nations Union, earnestly commending the League to " all the citizens of my Empire." His Majesty's strong championship of the League is of the greater interest because, after the Senate in Washington had, so far as the United States was concerned, wrecked the scheme their President Wilson had proposed and had largely carried through in Paris by his own exertions, the duty of leading the movement for the peaceful settlement of disputes fell on the British Empire.

At every one of the more important ceremonies connected with the victory of 1918 the King was present ; and, whether in St. Paul's Cathedral or the Guildhall, or in buildings with humbler traditions, he always maintained the character, to which his years were beginning to add a greater dignity still, of the father of his people.

In June 1921 the King went to Belfast to open the first Session of the Parliament of Northern Ireland. " I could not have allowed myself to give Ireland by deputy alone my earnest prayers and good wishes," he said.

He pleaded for the co-operation of every Irishman. " I speak from a full heart when I pray that my coming to Ireland to-day may prove to be the first step towards an end of strife." Then, his voice trembling with emotion, the King implored them to forgive and forget—to open up a new era of peace and goodwill.

In July the same year the King and Queen paid an interesting visit to the Channel Islands. He went, not as

H.M. KING EDWARD VIII.

H.R.H. THE DUKE OF YORK.

KING GEORGE *photographed for the first time in his uniform as Chief of the Royal Air Force, which he wore for the R.A.F. Jubilee Review.*

KING GEORGE *taking the salute during his review of the R.A.F. in Jubilee year.*

INSPECTING THE GUARD OF HONOUR.

KING GEORGE arriving in Rushmoor Arena for the great Army Review in 1935.

KING GEORGE TAKING THE SALUTE *during the Army Review. Behind him were his four sons.*

KING GEORGE'S LAST OFFICIAL GLIMPSE OF HIS ARMY, *during the grand Jubilee review in Rushmoor Arena. Thousands of troops, representing all branches of the Service, marched past in salute, and the ceremony was watched by a huge crowd.*

KING GEORGE GOING ON BOARD *his yacht* Victoria and Albert, *for the Jubilee Naval Review off Spithead.*

THE ROYAL YACHT *steaming down the lines of the assembled Fleet.*

THREE CHEERS FOR THE KING. *British battleships came from all parts of the world to take part in the Naval Review off Spithead to celebrate King George's Silver Jubilee.*

KING GEORGE GREETING REPRESENTATIVES *of the Fishing Fleet during the Naval Review.*

THE KING'S STEAM YACHT, *VICTORIA AND ALBERT*, *which he used for the Naval Review.*

A GROUP *taken aboard the* Victoria *and* Albert *in* 1935, *showing King George with the officers of the Royal yacht.*

King of Great Britain, but as Duke of Normandy.

The next year saw the King at his accustomed work at home except for visits to Belgium and to the cemeteries there and in France. On May 8 Their Majesties left London for Brussels. They placed a wreath on the spot where Nurse Cavell was shot. On May 11 the King went to Zeebrugge, inspected the Mole, and visited the scene of Sir Roger Keyes's famous destruction of the hornet's nest of German submarines.

The King then proceeded to Passchendaele, where 12,000 British soldiers rest in the greatest cemetery on the Western Front. With bowed head, and in silence, His Majesty rendered homage to this great multitude of his own most faithful subjects, and then proceeded to Ypres, through the Menin Gate. Just at the point which was so well known as "Hell Fire Corner" the Burgomaster received the Royal Party, who inspected the plans for the Menin Memorial.

At Terlincthun, in one of the finest speeches which His Majesty ever delivered, he once again commemorated and held up to everlasting remembrance the men who had died for the Empire.

About this time three marriages in the Royal Family were solemnised. On February 28, 1922, the King was present at the marriage of his only daughter, Princess Mary, to Viscount Lascelles, eldest son of the Earl of Harewood. The service took place in Westminster Abbey, and the King gave away his daughter.

Their Majesties' first grandson, the Hon. George Henry Hubert (now Viscount Lascelles), was born on February 7, 1923, and his brother, Their Majesties' second grandson, the Hon. Gerald David, on August 21, 1924.

On Thursday, April 26, 1923, the marriage of Prince Albert, who had been created Duke of York, to Lady Elizabeth Bowes-Lyon, daughter of the Earl and Countess of Strathmore, took place in the Abbey. In the same year, the King's niece, Princess Maud, married Lord Carnegie, the eldest son of the Earl of Southesk.

The years rolled on, bringing their private joys and sorrows, their public pleasures and anxieties. Always the King and his Consort increased the respect and affection with which they were regarded by their subjects. Only a few of their activities can be recorded. There was a visit to Italy in 1923, when they were entertained by the King and Queen at Rome, saw the Pope at the Vatican, and went to the British graves on the Asoiga Plateau and at other scenes of the War. It led to the formation of an Italian institute called "The Friends of Great Britain," which had the support of Signor Mussolini.

The successful British Empire Exhibition at Wembley was opened by the King in 1924, and in the following year Their Majesties attended the Consecration of Liverpool Cathedral—a stately pile which, even now, has not been quite completed.

The sympathy of the whole nation went out to his Majesty on the death of Queen Alexandra on November 20, 1925. His devotion to his mother was well known ; during the years of her widowhood he had never failed to pay her a daily visit or to write to her.

Changing social and political conditions on this side of St. George's Channel found the King ready to fulfil all their demands upon him. To him, the Sovereign in whose reign arose so many precedents, fell the duty of appointing the first Labour Prime Minister who has ever controlled the destinies of the English people. Mr. Ramsay MacDonald became Prime Minister.

Once again, for a little while, all eyes were turned towards the King. As a constitutional monarch, placed above all political parties, he gave his full confidence to his new advisers, and there was not even a momentary jar in the smooth working of the State machinery.

The Labour Ministry lasted scarcely a year, for, towards the end of 1924, the Liberals withdrew their support from the Government, and at the consequent General Election, the Conservatives were given a commanding majority over all parties.

But the precedent was, in spite of its short duration, of great significance. In no respect was it more significant than in the proof which it gave of the King's ability to work with and earn the respect and affection of Labour advisers ; and those who were admitted to his intimate acquaintance say that he was never seen to better advantage than when reaffirming, as he frequently did, his personal admiration and regard for the many Labour leaders with whom he had been brought into close contact. That he worked easily with them was in keeping with his whole character and with his ideal of a genuinely national kingship.

The defeat of the Labour Government at the polls was particularly severe, and Mr. Baldwin returned to power, supported by an immense majority in the House of Commons. But though the political verdict of the election had been so decisive, the succeeding years were marked by growing industrial unrest which culminated in the general strike of 1926.

The King shared to the full the refusal of his people to take this dark event tragically, and so soon as it was over exercised the full weight of his authority in the direction of securing the pacification of minds and tempers. In a message to the nation on May 12, he appealed for the elimination of bitterness, recalled how steady and how orderly the country had remained under so severe a trial, and urged that the task of making good the mischief done should be undertaken by a united people.

The message was taken to heart, and though no efforts served to avert all the consequences of deepening industrial depression during subsequent years, neither King nor people were again subjected to the " extreme anxiety " of organised industrial strife.

In the preceding month Princess Elizabeth, daughter of the Duke and Duchess of York, had been born, Their Majesties being awakened between three and four o'clock on April 21 to receive the news of the birth of their first granddaughter. Princess Margaret Rose, the second daughter of the Duke and Duchess of York, was born on August 21, 1930.

III

Perhaps at this stage in the story of the life of King George the Fifth, it would be well to consider the important constitutional changes that took place during his reign. They are significant not only in their development of that great British Commonwealth of Nations, but they also have their importance upon the Throne to-day on which is seated King Edward VIII.

In *The Life and Letters of Walter Page*, who was the Ambassador of the United States to England during the Great War, there is an account of an interesting smoking-room chat with King George.

"He talked about himself," says Page, "and his position as King. One of the remarks of the King was : ' Knowing the difficulties of a limited monarch, I thank Heaven I am spared being an absolute one.'

"He went on," Page proceeds, "to enumerate the large number of things he was obliged to do, and the little power that he had, not at all in a tone of complaint but as a merely impersonal explanation."

The reign of King George will be notable for this—that in it a perfect constitutional adjustment of the monarchy to its contemporary environment, political and social, was effected. And it was effected for all time.

The King is sometimes called the crowned President of the Republic. That is no more than a fanciful description of his office. The government of the country is monarchical in form and democratic in practice. What George V really was—as the political events of his reign established—was a Democratic King.

For fifteen centuries there have been kings in Britain, and for more than three hundred years there has been a single Kingship. True, there has been an English revolution. Charles I was beheaded, and Cromwell assumed a dictatorship over the country. But on his death, the monarchical system was accepted again and has continued ever since.

Yet, as Mr. John Buchan has said, "in the last two hundred years, while the Throne has lost in definable powers, it has gained in significance. There have been wise monarchs, and some not so wise, but the inherent and accumulated majesty of the office has increased."

In short, the Throne has come closer to the lives of the common people. The majesty of the King is no longer the awful majesty of the Middle Ages. The King is known to his people, moves among them, speaks to them and is now looked upon as the real defender of their liberties against the increasing powers of the State.

It was this instinct of being defender of the people's rights that was seen so strongly in the character of King George V. And when Mr. Stanley Baldwin referred to the reign as "the most difficult quarter of a century in which a monarch has ever sat on the Throne," he doubtless had the Constitutional problems in mind.

In the first place, King George had to set his own position right in relation to the people of this country. Although the blood of King George was mainly German, it can safely be said that no more English King ever sat on the Throne. Despite the origin of the Coburg family, in its small principality on the fringe of the Thuringian Forest, that branch which came to England soon shed their German trappings. King George was essentially an Englishman, and both by early training and environment soon revealed himself as more English than the English. Throughout his reign he was regarded as the very apotheosis of the English gentleman.

During the Great War the King took a very popular step when he decided to

EIGHT THOUSAND REPRESENTATIVES *of Britain's police forces paraded before King George in Hyde Park during Jubilee celebrations. It was the first Royal police review ever held.*

KING GEORGE *talking to Lord Jellicoe on board the* Britannia *during Cowes Regatta in* 1935. *It was the last visit they ever paid to Cowes. Lord Jellicoe's death preceded the King's by a few weeks.*

adopt the name of " Windsor," for himself and his family, and at the same time divested himself of all German titles and dignities.

The official Proclamation—a most important one for this country and the Royal Family—was as follows :

" Declaring that the name of Windsor is to be Borne by His Royal House and Family and Relinquishing the Use of All German Titles and Dignities.
" GEORGE R.I.

" Whereas We, having taken into consideration the Name and Title of Our Royal House and Family, have determined that henceforth Our House and Family shall be styled and known as the House and Family of Windsor :

" And whereas We have further determined for Ourselves and for and on behalf of Our descendants and all other descendants of Our Grandmother Queen Victoria of blessed and glorious memory to relinquish and discontinue the use of all German Titles and Dignities ;

" And whereas We have declared these Our determinations in Our Privy Council :

" Now, therefore, We, out of Our Royal Will and Authority do hereby declare and announce that as from the date of this Our Royal Proclamation Our House and Family shall be styled and known as the House and Family of Windsor, and that all the descendants in the male line of Our said Grandmother Queen Victoria who are subjects of these Realms, other than female descendants who may marry or may have married, shall bear the said name of Windsor :

" And do hereby further declare and announce that We for Ourselves and

for and on behalf of Our descendants and all other the descendants of Our said Grandmother Queen Victoria who are subjects of these Realms, relinquish and enjoin the discontinuance of the use of the Degrees, Styles, Dignities, Titles and Honours of Dukes and Duchesses of Saxony and Princes and Princesses of Saxe-Coburg and Gotha, and all other German Degrees, Styles, Dignities, Titles, Honours and Appellations to Us or to them heretofore belonging or appertaining.

" Given at Our Court at Buckingham Palace, this
" Seventeenth day of July, in the year of Our Lord One thousand nine hundred and seventeen, and in the Eighth year of Our Reign.
" GOD SAVE THE KING."

Some years later, consequent upon discussions by the Imperial Conference, there was another Proclamation which set forth the title and relations of the King to the Empire. It has been emphasised throughout the course of this history that the British Commonwealth of Nations is binding only in its common symbol of Kingship. The King of England is also King of Canada, King of Australia, King of South Africa, and Emperor of India. The suggestion that King Edward VIII shall be crowned in each of the Dominions is based upon this Constitutional fact.

It was in May 1927 that a Royal Proclamation set out the new style and title to be used by His Majesty, consequent on the recommendation of the Imperial Conference of the previous year. For the words " United Kingdom of Great Britain and Ireland " in the Royal title were substituted the words " Great Britain, Ireland," thus making His Majesty's description : "George V, by the Grace of God of Great Britain, Ireland, and of the British Dominions beyond the Seas, King, Defender of the Faith, Emperor of India."

But on the very day that King George ascended the Throne, he was faced by a political crisis in Britain which challenged the powers of the King himself. The House of Commons had definitely challenged the powers of the House of Lords. The Asquith Ministry refused to advise a Dissolution without a " hypothetical " promise from the King that if the country supported the Government, sufficient Peers would be created to carry the Parliament Bill (already passed by the Commons) through the Lords.

It was a cruel dilemma. What exactly happened when the Ministers (on November 16) pointed this pistol at the King's head there is now only one man alive who can say : and that man—Lord Crewe—admitted (in the House of Lords) that to him the whole business was " odious."

The sequel is public history. Great Britain, again consulted in December, again returned an ambiguous answer, but the Irish members enabled the Government to carry their Bill through the Commons, and the Lords surrendered. The Parliament Bill became law.

Another crisis—deeply distressing to the King—almost immediately supervened. The Irish Nationalists had not supported the Parliament Bill for nothing. They claimed their pound of flesh. A Home Rule Bill passed the Commons. Ulster refused to accept it, and armed. The Nationalists also armed. In the summer of 1914 Civil War threatened. The King summoned a Conference of Party leaders

to Buckingham Palace, and most solemnly adjured them to reach a compromise. They failed ; civil war was averted only by the outbreak of the World War.

Again during the Great War, the King exercised his powers as head of the Fighting Forces.

" First of the Allied Chiefs to realise the value of unity of Command, and the one to bring it into being, was the King of England, George the Fifth."

This is a passage from the unpublished diaries of the late Marshal Foch, and it is confirmed by a note found among the papers of the War-time French Premier, Georges Clemenceau.

In amplifying notes Foch reveals that King George had first of all expressed in strong terms his conviction that the weakness of the Allies lay in the lack of cohesion between the different armies, and that the only remedy was in some form of unity of Command.

" The political as well as the army chiefs of the Allied Powers in the West, with the exception of Belgium, would not hear of unity that did not mean handing the command over to them.

" King George made many helpful suggestions for overcoming the difficulties, but nothing came of them until the fateful spring and summer of 1918, when King George had won over the more important of the British political chiefs to the view that for the Allies the choice was between unity of command and defeat."

Then follows an account of the failure of the politicians to convince the army chiefs of the same fact and of the arrival of a crisis, when there was the possibility of the British General Staff resigning *en masse* if French

KING GEORGE AND QUEEN MARY *photographed with their granddaughter, Princess Margaret Rose, during a visit to Scotland in September* 1935.

A CHARMING INFORMAL PICTURE *of King George and Queen Mary.*

command was imposed on the British Army.

It was at this critical stage that the King appeared on the scene once more and made the move that brought unity of command into being.

He made known to Sir Douglas Haig and the other chiefs his firm conviction that the cause of the Allies could best be served by accepting the leadership of Foch.

With this definite expression of opinion from the Sovereign and the Chief of the Army, the General Staff could no longer stand in the way, and Sir Douglas Haig's famous letter, placing himself and his troops under the orders of the Generalissimo, followed.

" It was the King of England who saved the unity of command when it was menaced, and, in saving it, he saved the Allies from defeat," is the comment of Clemenceau.

Foch's comment is : " I say nothing of what I am told was the intervention of the King when I personally was involved, but I do say without fear of contradiction that his foresight and firmness on the question of unity of command brought to the Allies victory instead of the defeat that menaced them."

The choice of a Prime Minister is, within strict limits, still part of the Royal Prerogative. King George definitely exercised that Prerogative when in May 1922 he appointed Mr. Baldwin in preference to Lord Curzon or anybody else. There was not, indeed, a wide choice open to the King, but there was some choice, and he exercised it.

But perhaps the greatest part played by King George in the history of this country occurred in 1931, when Great Britain was on the verge of bankruptcy. Sir Charles Petrie, in his book on *Monarchy*, has emphasised the seriousness of the situation.

" At this moment when the nation was vainly looking round for a Mussolini to save it from the consequences of its own, and its chosen leaders', blunders, the King stepped into the breach. When the crisis occurred he was at Balmoral, and as soon as it was announced that he was coming to London a sigh of relief went up from the whole country ; the long-awaited chief had made his appearance, and in the person of the King. Once again monarchy had saved the day when democracy had failed.

" Those who may be inclined to dispute this assertion would do well to reflect upon what would have happened had Great Britain been a republic in August 1931. The President would either have been a colourless nonentity or a violent partisan. If the former, he would never have dared to adopt a definite policy of his own, and at a time when every hour was of importance if catastrophe was to be avoided, days, and probably weeks, would have been wasted in consultations with the various party leaders before a new administration could have been formed. Had the President been a partisan he would not have possessed the confidence of the nation, and as the probability is that he would have been a Socialist, his chief concern would most likely have been, not the future of the Empire, but that of his political associates.

" Whether King George had foreseen that such action on his part might one day be necessary it is, of course, impossible to say, but he showed from the first that he fully realised that immediate decision was essential if the situation were to be saved. It was many a long year since a British sovereign had intervened so decisively in domestic politics, and when the country was asked to endorse his action it did so in a manner unprecedented in the national history.

" The published accounts of what happened at Buckingham Palace those August days of 1931 leave no doubt whatever that the formation of the National Government was primarily the work of the King. There was no new group to which he could turn, as the King of Italy had turned to the Fascists nine years before, and as all three parties were responsible for the perilous condition in which the country found itself, it was only right that all three should share the burden of restoring the situation.

" To have allowed Mr. MacDonald, Mr. Snowden, and Mr. Thomas to resign, and to have installed a purely Conservative administration would have been to have treated these three gentlemen with an indulgence which they certainly did not deserve. It is true that the formation of a ministry which was composed of the spendthrifts of all three parties appeared at first sight to be taking too literally the old tag about the reformed poacher making the best gamekeeper, but the Crown had no choice ; there was not a politician in the land who was not to some extent implicated, and the only thing the King could do was to form a composite Cabinet, and trust to himself and to his subjects to see that the erstwhile poachers did not lapse into their old habits.

" The sole alternative would have been to have called to power some national figure, if such a one could be found, outside the ranks of the politicians altogether, but in view of the fact that no one was specially indicated it would have been a very dubious experiment and had it been adopted the result would probably have been the same as in Spain during the government of General Primo de Rivera, when the old politicians unpatriotically refused to co-operate with the Prime Minister chosen by the King.

" King George has been accused of unconstitutional conduct, and the events of August 1931 have been described as a palace revolution. In reality nothing could be farther from the truth, and had His Majesty not acted as he did he would have been violating the Constitution. The settlement at the Revolution went a long way towards rendering the Crown powerless in face of the parties, but it did leave the monarchy some independent power, of which later sovereigns took advantage.

" The charge against the King is that he should have accepted the resignation of the Socialist Cabinet, and then sent for Mr. Baldwin to form a purely Conservative one. This accusation, needless to say, is made by Socialists of the Henderson-Lansbury persuasion, and it was brought after the Socialist rout at the General Election of 1931. Before that event the crisis was described as a ' banker's ramp,' the banks being presumed to be more unpopular than the monarchy with the electorate, and therefore the more profitable to attack.

" Upon every score the King acted in a perfectly constitutional manner. He believed that the only hope of restoring the situation lay in the formation of a non-party Government, and from

KING GEORGE AND QUEEN MARY, *with the Duchess of York, at the Command Variety Performance at the London Palladium in October 1935.*

THE WEDDING *of the Duke of Gloucester to Lady Alice Scott in November 1935. It was one of King George's last public appearances.*

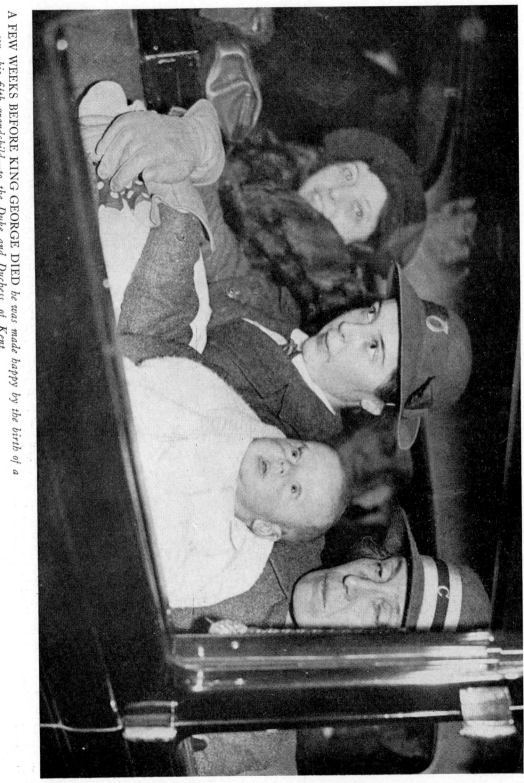

A FEW WEEKS BEFORE KING GEORGE DIED he was made happy by the birth of a son—his fifth grandchild—to the Duke and Duchess of Kent.

the beginning, he worked to this end.

The result of these trials and decisions in Statecraft proved that King George had decided that the monarchy, while lifted far above the nation, should also be the nation itself in its most characteristic form. Again, to quote Mr. John Buchan:

" The historian must record that the King has added to the duties of the Crown a graciousness which springs from his own character. He has given to ceremonial the bloom of friendliness. He has always possessed a high seriousness, and the note of faith and piety which he has often struck has not been the mere convention of his office.

" He has walked securely in more difficult constitutional paths than any of his immediate predecessors. He has faced courageously crises which imperilled both his people and his Throne. But, in addition to all this, he has diffused a spirit of simplicity and charity which has profoundly affected the national temper. His quick sympathy and kindliness have warmed the country, and done something to warm a chilly world.

" When nerve was breaking his steadfastness has restored it, and when strife was fermenting he has spoken the healing word. The power of the Throne lies in what it is; but the authority of the King lies both in what he is, and in what he has done. With the Queen and his family to aid him, he had made Britain not only a nation but a household."

IV

We now enter upon the period during which the millions of people in this Commonwealth of Nations showed, in no uncertain fashion, their devotion and loyalty to King George.

The whole nation was plunged into a long period of acute anxiety by the serious illness of His Majesty. It began in November, 1928, when it was announced that the King was suffering from a cold and some fever. It is believed that following a slight chill contracted at Sandringham, the King's condition was aggravated by standing before the Cenotaph in the cold, damp weather of Armistice Day.

By the beginning of December bulletins were being issued twice daily and posted in a frame outside Buckingham Palace, where they were read anxiously by large crowds. On December 3 came the grave statement : " There is a decline in the strength of the heart, which causes anxiety."

A Council of State was appointed on the following day, the Queen and the Prince of Wales—who was hurrying back from Central Africa—being included among its members.

An operation for the drainage of the right side of the chest was performed by Sir Hugh Rigby on December 12, and one of the bulletins issued was signed by six medical men.

Slow improvement was recorded for some time after this, but on December 28 it was reported that there had been a check in the progress made and that the King " had a very narrow margin of safety."

A long and anxious struggle followed, but slow and steady improvement took place, and towards the end of January came the patient's first published message since the commencement of his illness. It was to the House Governor of Middlesex Hospital, where the

Queen was laying the foundation-stone of a new Nurses' home, and in it the King said his illness had " brought him to appreciate more deeply than ever before the value of medical science and of devoted nursing."

On February 9 the Royal patient was moved to Craigwell House, Bognor. He was taken thither in a motor ambulance, and thousands of silent sympathisers lined the route.

Thenceforward his progress, though slow, was sure. By the end of March he was able to spend part of his time on the sea-wall, whence he acknowledged the greetings of the crowds who gathered on the beach, and he seemed to gain strength daily.

A touching message of an intimate and personal kind from the King to his people signalised his recovery. It was dated April 22, and, as the *Morning Post* said at the time, revealed in every phrase the close human relationship existing between His Majesty and his subjects—" a relationship as near and dear as that between members of the same household." The message included these passages :

" In looking back on my long illness and recovery, my heart is full of thankfulness of far deeper origin than any mere sense of relief.

" I have been brought back from the danger and weariness of the past months by the wonderful skill of my Doctors, Surgeons, and Nurses. And help has come from another source of strength ; as month after month went by I learned of the widespread and loving solicitude with which the Queen and I were surrounded. I was able to picture to myself the crowds of friends waiting and watching at my gates, and to think of the still greater number of those who, in every part of the Empire, were remembering me with prayers and good wishes. The realisation of this has been among the most vivid experiences of my life.

" It was an encouragement beyond description to feel that my constant and earnest desire had been granted—the desire to gain the confidence and affection of my people."

The King feelingly referred also to the sympathy shown him by unknown friends in other countries, and said he longed to believe it possible that his experiences might soon appear no longer exceptional ; when the national anxiety of all peoples " shall be felt as a common source of human sympathy and a common claim on human friendship."

A Thank-offering Fund for the King's recovery was inaugurated by a gift of £105,000 from " Audax," the money to be devoted to King Edward's Hospital Fund for London. The King, the Queen, and the Prince of Wales were among those who contributed, and when the Fund was closed in the following December no less a sum than £689,597 had been subscribed.

When His Majesty left Craigwell House for Windsor in the middle of May he was joyfully acclaimed by crowds who had gathered along the route. He returned to London, apparently fully recovered, at the end of June. Memorable scenes of loyalty and affection marked his drive to Buckingham Palace, whence he issued a message expressing his heartfelt gratitude.

At the beginning of July, accompanied by the Queen, he attended a service of thanksgiving (which was broadcast) in Westminster Abbey.

Shortly afterwards, he had to submit to another operation, owing to the formation of an internal abscess, and portions of two ribs were removed. Happily he soon recovered, and in the middle of August was able to hold a Council at Buckingham Palace. Not long afterwards he was so much his old self that he could enjoy motoring, fishing, and shooting at Sandringham.

In April 1931 the King was again taken ill. He had motored to Windsor with the Queen on a cold, bleak day and had apparently sustained a chill. On the 6th it was announced that he was kept indoors by a slight cold, and on the following day it became known that the cold had developed into an attack of sub-acute bronchitis. Happily, his health improved, and in May, after celebrating the 21st anniversary of his Accession to the Throne, he was able to return to London.

Between these two relapses His Majesty was able to open the Five-Power Naval Conference at St. James's Palace. His speech, delivered in a clear, ringing voice, was broadcast. There was much unemployment at the time, and he set a good example by ordering five new Daimler cars, explaining that his object was to stimulate British industry. In July he opened the new dock at Glasgow, and five days later the new King George Hospital at Ilford.

The year 1931 also brought with it a grave national crisis, with the making of which the King was dramatically associated; and though the event may still be too recent to be viewed in its proper perspective, history will probably record it as a striking instance of perfectly correct and yet decisive action by a constitutional Sovereign.

Throughout the year the industrial depression had been deepening and spreading through other countries so far relatively immune. The political and financial embarrassments of the Labour Government had been becoming more acute. The report of the May Committee showed enormous deficits in the Budget in prospect, and during August there developed what amounted to a flight from the pound. The Government, or some members of it, realised that drastic steps to restore confidence were necessary, but proved unable to agree upon a definite programme.

The King, who had been at Balmoral, returned by special train to London on Sunday, August 23. There he at once engaged in consultation with all the party leaders, Mr. Baldwin and Sir Herbert Samuel having been sent for "on the Prime Minister's advice." The result was their agreement to form a National Government, and for this solution of an awkward and dangerous situation the nation had nobody to thank more than the King himself.

It must be pointed out that this step involved not the slightest interference with policy by the Crown. The King kept strictly to his constitutional function of suggesting an association of Ministers by whom he could be advised. It is true that later he helped them in an unpleasant and difficult task by reducing the Civil List by £50,000, but that only showed his willingness, as always, to share in everything which affected his people, and did not mark any Royal inspiration of policy.

So the crisis was overpast. The Monarch's intervention, not less than his own sacrifice to the national emergency, had a great share in the calming

One of the happiest of events of the year 1934 was the announcement in the " Court Circular " of August 28, of the betrothal of the fourth son of the King and Queen, Prince George.

The bride was Princess Marina, third of the three daughters of Prince and Princess Nicolas of Greece. Her father is a brother of the late King Constantine, and her mother was the Grand Duchess Helene of Russia. Her grandfather was the late King George of Greece, brother of the late Queen Alexandra.

Princess Marina was born in Athens on November 30, 1906. She was educated in Paris, and paid fairly frequent visits to London. The engagement took place on Prince George's holiday, spent with Prince and Princess Paul of Jugoslavia, the sister and brother-in-law of Princess Marina.

Princess Marina received an enthusiastic welcome on arriving with her parents in London, en route for Balmoral, on September 16. The King and Queen gave her an affectionate greeting next day at Balmoral Castle, where she and her parents remained until September 23.

The wedding took place in Westminster Abbey on November 29. Here again, broadcast played an historic part. The whole ceremony in the Abbey, including the bride's responses, was heard by millions of listeners. Driving from the Abbey, Prince George and his bride received a tumultuous welcome from the huge crowds. The cheering reached its crescendo outside Buckingham Palace, where the happy couple, surrounded by the Royal Family, appeared on the balcony nodding and smiling to the enthusiastic crowds. It was a splendid augury for the wave

of the public mind ; and in the following February, His Majesty, acknowledging addresses from the Convocation of Canterbury and York, remarked on the " fortitude of his people in the face of difficulties." " This," he added, " had shown the world that the spirit of unity and mutual service which shone so brightly during the miseries of war, still lives in their hearts, ready to be rekindled in time of national emergency."

It was in 1931, one of the first acts of the new Parliament, that the Statute of Westminster was passed. It revolutionised the constitutional position of the King towards the Governments outside the United Kingdom. Up to then he had acted upon the advice of his Ministers here ; now the Governments of all the Dominions Overseas advise His Majesty on matters affecting their own countries. This momentous change was the result of resolutions of the Imperial Conference in 1928 and 1930—passed on the initiative of the Irish Free State and the Union of South Africa.

In 1932, and the following two years, many ceremonial, and memorable, duties fell to the lot of the King and his Consort.

His Majesty opened the World Economic Conference, to which sixty-six countries sent delegates. He was always deeply interested in functions which demonstrated the march of scientific endeavour—such, for instance, as when he and the Queen sailed down Southampton Water into the largest graving-dock in the world ; or when, at Liverpool, he opened a tunnel, driven for two miles under the Mersey, or when the Queen, in his presence, launched the huge Cunard-White Star liner named after her.

A NUN PRAYING *outside the Lodge gates at Sandringham for the recovery of King George.*

THE SCENE AT BUCKINGHAM PALACE *when the announcement of King George's death was posted.*

A FAVOURITE PHOTOGRAPH—AND A FAVOURITE PONY. This was the last photograph to be taken of the well-beloved monarch with his favourite pony "Jock." It is said that King George himself preferred this informal picture to any other.

THE ROYAL STANDARD *at half-mast on Windsor Castle on the news that King George was dead.*

READING THE PROCLAMATION *of the Accession of King Edward VIII on the death of his father.*

THE WHITE ENSIGN *being lowered to half-mast aboard the Victory on the news of King George's death.*